Wild Sweets

CHOCOLATE

from the atelier of
DOMINIQUE & CINDY DUBY

Savory | Sweet | Bites | Drinks

wild sweets
CHOCOLATE

foreword by
CHARLIE TROTTER

whitecap

Copyright © 2007 by Dominique & Cindy Duby

Whitecap Books

All rights reserved. No part of this publication may be reproduced, stored in a retrieval system, or transmitted in any form or by any means, electronic, mechanical, photocopying, recording or otherwise, without the prior written permission of the publisher. For more information, contact Whitecap Books, 351 Lynn Avenue, North Vancouver, British Columbia, Canada V7J 2C4. Visit our website at www.whitecap.ca.

All recommendations are made without guarantee on the part of the author or Whitecap Books Ltd. The author and publisher disclaim any liability in connection with the use of this information.

Edited by Nadine Boyd
Jacket and interior design by Linda Mitsui
Jacket and interior photography by Dominique & Cindy Duby
For other photography credits see page 202

Printed and bound in China.

Library and Archives Canada Cataloguing in Publication

Duby, Dominique, 1961-
    Wild sweets : chocolate : savory, sweet, bites,
drinks / Dominique Duby.

Includes index.
ISBN 978-1-55285-910-0
ISBN 1-55285-910-X

    1. Cookery (Chocolate). I. Title.

TX767.C5D82 2007   641.6'374   C2007-901774-6

The publisher acknowledges the financial support of the Government of Canada through the Book Publishing Industry Development Program (BPIDP) and the province of British Columbia through the Book Publishing Tax Credit.

contents

Dining is and always was
a great artistic
opportunity
- Frank Lloyd Wright

Foreword

stu·pen·dous

Pronunciation: /stuːˈpendəs,ˈstjuː-/ Causing astonishment or wonder. Awesome, marvelous, of amazing size or greatness, tremendous.

That is the first word that comes to mind merely fifteen pages into Dominique and Cindy Duby's incredible new book, *Wild Sweets Chocolate*. It is simply stupendous! I was not sure how they were ever going to outdo their glorious first work, *Wild Sweets*, but they have done so in definitive fashion. I have always maintained that the greatest chefs have an equal affinity for the sweet or dessert part of the meal, and likewise, the greatest pastry chefs have a love and use for all things savory. I think though, that Dominique and Cindy have downright blurred the line in terms of melding food stuffs that typically would be categorized as sweet or savory. Their other virtuoso performance is that they have taken "the Food of the Gods," chocolate, and have flawlessly woven it through every preparation in the book.

As chefs worldwide continue to push the culinary envelope, stand old ideas on their head, fuse this culture's cuisine with that, toil in laboratories, incorporate the latest technologies, consult food scientists, and debate each other at gastronomic summits, it is the rare few that truly break through with important and lasting ideas. The creations contained in *Wild Sweets Chocolate* are fluid and provocative, yet have depth and eloquence that is only found in the hands of those that have a true mastery and profound understanding of their craft.

Another extraordinary thing you will discover in these pages is that Dominique and Cindy accentuate texture as an incredibly important part of each preparation—for some chefs this comes as merely an afterthought. And where to start with the visuals—I would say nothing shy of tour de force! Plus there is the added benefit of seeing the dish plated two ways, even emphasizing different uses of the ingredients for the exact same preparation. Unheard of! I almost wince to think of the next Duby cookbook … at this rate, it may make the rest of us want to give it all up.

Congratulations Dominique and Cindy, you have produced a highly original and utterly profound work of art! Three cheers to you both!

Charlie

CHARLIE TROTTER

introduction

Chocolate is the ingredient of choice when it comes to designing and preparing sweets. This book provides fresh, unique, and modern ideas for plated desserts, sweet drinks, and petit-fours (which we call bites). The unique nature of these recipes comes from the fact that chocolate is used in every one of them—even the savory ones. While chocolate is traditionally used by some countries in select savory dishes, such as mole poblano (a turkey stew with bittersweet chocolate), we have taken the concept of chocolate cuisine to a broader spectrum.

Preparing fish, shellfish, or meat dishes with chocolate may seem unconventional, but once it's understood how to incorporate its exclusive taste profile and characteristics, chocolate is an equally incredible component in savory preparations as it is in sweet.

In order to design dishes with non-conventional flavor combinations —such as chocolate with savory foods—it is valuable to understand how we perceive and taste food. Although the following material is not exclusively related to chocolate, it provides a broader understanding of food design, which is necessary when preparing and serving savory chocolate-based dishes.

The process of flavor perception is multi-sensory and distinctly individual. Each person sees, hears, and tastes differently. Key influencing factors in food appreciation include: memory, culture, and context. An individual may have loved a particular food as a child, yet no longer finds that food appealing. Eating grasshoppers may be considered disgusting to some, but is a delicacy to others. Smelling a dirty sock might repel some, yet a similar odor within cheeses has no effect on others.

To the inexperienced, the idea of chocolate cuisine may be visualized as a piece of meat served with a sweet chocolate sauce. This misconception is due to the memory of chocolate classically being used in a sweet context. When designing and presenting savory chocolate dishes, it's best to think of chocolate as a spice rather than a main ingredient—an underlying element rather than an overtly bold one. Be aware that too much chocolate can make a savory dish too sweet and cloying.

Contrary to popular belief, taste (what is typically referred to as flavor) is actually more of a matter of smell. Research demonstrates that up to 80% of what we perceive as taste is actually perceived by our sense of smell. Aroma is registered in the olfactory epithelium, which contains hundreds of receptors. Aromatic components in food are released during mastication and these vapors are related to the speed of mastication as well as the length of time the food is masticated. The longer a food is masticated, the more vapors (flavor) are released into the nose. When you eat fresh pineapple, you taste the sweetness of the fruit, but the flavor associated with pineapple is actually the aromatic makeup of the fruit recognized through smell. So, it's best to think of taste in terms of what we perceive when a food is in contact with our taste buds. Whereas flavor should be thought of as the combination between what we taste and what we smell.

What we taste are really only four different types of true taste perceptions: sour, sweet, salt, and bitter. (Recent research in the field of neuro-physiology points also to a fifth category, "umami.") We register these tastes through thousands of taste buds, which bind to a specific structure of a taste molecule. Sweet receptors recognize different types of sugars; sour receptors respond to acids; salt receptors respond to metal ions; and bitter receptors are triggered by alkaloids. It was thought for a long time that the tongue is broken into four taste areas: sweet on the tip, bitter at the back, sour on the sides, and salt along the edges. Today's findings provide evidence that the tongue can actually taste all the stimuli in any one area.

Aroma plays a very important role as far as flavor compatibility. In many cases, certain foods go well together (such as fish and chips or strawberries and cream) because they have a key aroma molecule in common. This food pairing approach is becoming increasingly popular by identifying and combining certain foods that contain the same aromatic molecules. Examples of same aromatic molecules in the context of chocolate are caviar and white chocolate, green peppercorns and dark chocolate, or caramelized cauliflower and cocoa. Understanding flavor pairing is of particular value in chocolate cuisine. One can start with established sweet flavor pairings, such as chocolate with berries, port, nuts, or ginger. These can be transformed into a savory dish like Duck with Spiced Almond Crumb, Stewed Cherries, and Chocolate Port Reduction (see page 62).

Flavor within a dish is acquired in two ways: through the addition of an aroma or through the initiation of a chemical reaction. Fresh herbs and spices provide aromatic elements, the same as good quality extracts like vanilla, mint, or bitter almond. Typically, products in their natural state provide superior and more complex results than aromas. This is largely due to the fact that many aromas simply don't contain as many aromatic molecules. However, there are some ingredients that prove the contrary, such as vanilla. A controlled testing showed that artificial vanilla was preferred to natural vanilla extract. This reveals how distinctly individual the process of flavor perception is, and potentially references the fact that most people grew up in households where artificial vanilla was used to make celebratory sweets, forever linking the artificial flavor and feel-good memories. The other option for flavor is chemical reactions. These are typically initiated when several components come into contact with one another for a certain amount of time at a certain temperature. For example, the Maillard reaction is initiated when amino acids and carbohydrates are heated together. It produces pleasant aromas or flavors such as the crust of baked bread, browning of meat, roasting of coffee beans et cetera. The process of making chocolate also involves a reaction through the roasting of the cocoa beans, which provides another flavor dimension to savory dishes.

Temperature has a great effect on food. A bitter flavor, for example, is less noticeable when the food is hot than at room temperature. As a test, make a bitter brew of coffee and compare the taste of the hot versus

the cold version. Another way to manipulate bitterness is to add a little salt to a bitter element (i.e. bitter dark chocolate sauce). This can make it taste, or at least be perceived to taste, sweeter. Sweet flavors are less noticeable when cold than warm. For example, take a sip of soda pop at room temperature versus the same drink cold from the refrigerator. A good quality, high cocoa percentage dark chocolate is typically quite bitter, whereas white and milk chocolate can be somewhat sweet. By playing with temperature, white or milk chocolate preparations can be made to taste less sweet when served cold. As you can see, temperature is particularly important when cooking with chocolate.

The form of chocolate used in a preparation can drastically influence how a dish will taste and look. Using chocolate in a bar form is one option, but the various components that make up chocolate are also available individually, each providing distinct characteristics with taste and texture benefits. Cocoa nibs, for example, are dried, roasted cocoa beans, which are then cracked into nibs. This pure form of chocolate is unsweetened and perfect to make clear chocolate infusions or broth. Unlike chocolate in bar form, cocoa nibs add a chocolate flavor, but don't change the appearance or consistency of a dish. Cocoa nibs are

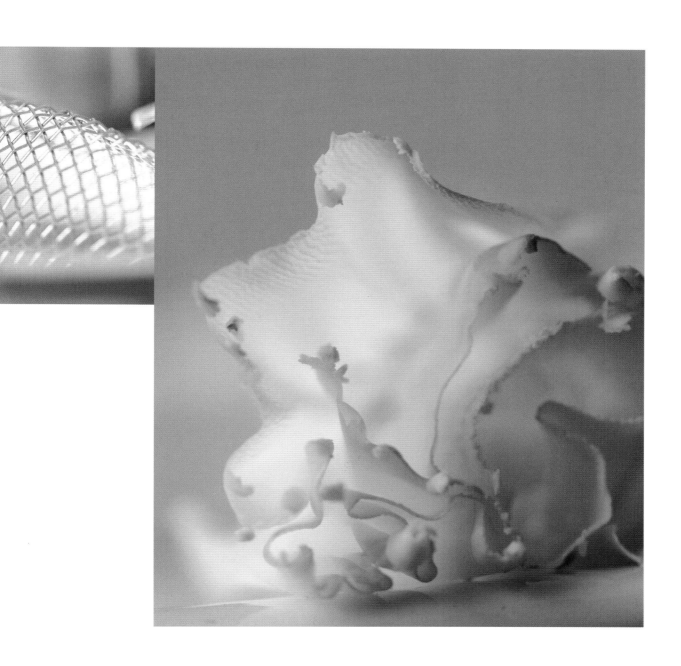

also great to add texture to a sweet or savory dish. Another variation is cocoa butter, which can be use instead of (or in conjunction with) other fats to provide distinct flavor profiles in sauces (see page 160 for more details on cocoa butter). Cocoa powder (sweetened or unsweetened) offers a richer chocolate flavor than chocolate in bar form. Cocoa powder is great to use as part of a rub or to intensify a sauce or braising liquid. For further information on chocolate's uses in sweets, please refer to our first book, *Wild Sweets: Exotic Dessert & Wine Pairings.*

At its roots, cooking is similar to performing a laboratory experiment. Cooking involves the combination of a range of ingredients in various forms (liquid, solid, gas), exposed to a sequence of chemical reactions (such as caramelization or gelatinization), for a given amount of time, at a specific temperature. One of the main reasons cooking failures occur is because one is more preoccupied with the effect rather than the cause, which one tends to implement automatically. Understanding how these elements (liquid, solid, and gas) react in different conditions is the key to consistent results.

Our dishes are abundant with modern tastes and textures that stimulate all the senses. In the Sweet and Savory recipes, we have provided two options for each dish; one is intended as an elegant version for special occasions while the other (denoted with the "e" symbol) is intended for simpler, everyday meals. For best results in reproducing our recipes we recommend the use of a scale for precise measurement.

At Wild Sweets, we implement a philosophy of "culinary constructivism" inspired by our studies as educators. Constructivism is a philosophy of learning based on the premise that we construct our own understanding of the world by reflecting on our experiences. As such, we want this book to be a source of inspiration for you. We urge you to construct and experiment based on your individual preferences and creativity.

Research is to see
what everybody has seen
and to think what nobody else has thought

– Albert Szent-Gyorgyi

The key to success in food design is defining an identity
– it is the result of a careful creative process and its rationale.

savory

shellfish | S_1S

CRAB
White Chocolate Hollandaise
Potato Brulée | Hot Celery Gelée

PRAWN
Orange Chili Chocolate Mayonnaise
Wakame Salad | Prawn Meringue

SHRIMP
Capers Mincemeat Chocolate Jam
Mango Carpaccio | Cucumber Gelée

SCALLOP
Baked Grapefruit Chocolate Cheesecake
Asparagus Ribbons | Bacon Porcini Crumble

CRAB | White Chocolate Hollandaise | Potato Brulée | Hot Celery Gelée

SERVES 8

Potato Brulée

1 lb (500 g) russet potatoes,
   peeled and cubed

½ cup (150 g) goat cheese

salt, pepper, and freshly grated
   nutmeg to taste

2 large eggs

½ cup (125 mL) whipping cream

1 Tbsp (15 mL) Gelatin Mix
   (see page 185)

½ cup (125 mL) Vegetable Stock
   (see page 190)

1½ tsp (7.5 mL) agar powder

Line a 6 x 8 inch (15 x 20 cm) baking pan with plastic wrap (bottom and sides). Place the potatoes in a pot of cold salted water, place the pot over high heat, and boil until the potatoes are tender. Drain the liquid and pass the potatoes through a fine sieve or rice mill into a bowl. Add the goat cheese, salt, pepper, and nutmeg and mix until well combined.

In a separate, heatproof bowl combine the eggs and whipping cream. Place the bowl over a double boiler and whisk until the mixture thickens and reaches 185°F (85°C). Add the Gelatin Mix and whisk until dissolved.

In a tall and narrow container, blend the Vegetable Stock and agar with an immersion blender until well combined. Transfer into a saucepan and bring to a boil. Remove from the heat, immediately add the egg and whipping cream mixture, and whisk until well combined. Add to the potato and goat cheese mixture, quickly fold with a rubber spatula, and transfer into the plastic lined baking pan. Smooth the mixture with an offset spatula and let it set in the refrigerator.

 version _____

Simply make Potato Purée by omitting the vegetable stock/agar/gelatin mix step and just adding the whipping cream to the potato and cheese mixture. Season to taste, and keep warm.

Hot Celery Gelée

½ lb (250 g) crab meat, cooked
  (chunks and claws are best)

¾ cup (175 mL) celery juice
  (see Vegetable Juice, page 186)

3 Tbsp (45 mL) pink grapefruit juice

pinch ascorbic acid (optional)

½ tsp (2.5 mL) agar powder

1½ tsp (7.5 mL) Gelatin Mix
  (see page 185)

Preheat the oven to 200°F (95°C). Line a 6 x 8 inch (15 x 20 cm) heatproof shallow container with plastic wrap (bottom and sides). Arrange the pieces of crab on the bottom of the container and place into the preheated oven for a few minutes.

Meanwhile, pour the celery and grapefruit juice into a tall and narrow container. Add the ascorbic acid (if using) and agar powder and blend with an immersion blender until well combined. Transfer the mixture into a saucepan, bring to a boil, and continue cooking until the mixture begins to thicken. Add the Gelatin Mix, stir to dissolve, and immediately strain over the crab. Let this set at room temperature for 5 to 10 minutes. You can store in the refrigerator until ready to use.

Braised Celery Ribs

8 stalks celery, filaments removed

1 Tbsp (15 g) butter

1 Tbsp (15 mL) olive oil

1 Tbsp (15 mL) freshly squeezed
  grapefruit juice

2 tsp (10 mL) corn syrup

1 tsp (5 mL) celery seeds (optional)

½ cup (125 mL) Vegetable Stock
  (see page 190)

salt and pepper to taste

Cut the celery stalks into 1½ inch (4 cm) sticks. Bring the butter, oil, grapefruit juice, corn syrup, celery seeds and vegetable stock to a boil in a saucepan. Reduce the heat to minimum, add the celery stalks and season to taste. Cover the saucepan and heat until the stalks are cooked but have not lost their shape (10 to 15 minutes). Alternately, cook in a sealed bag in a 150°F (65°C) agitated water bath (see page 36). Keep warm until ready to serve.

White Chocolate Hollandaise

⅔ cup (150 mL) freshly squeezed
  grapefruit juice

1 tsp (5 mL) xanthan gum

1 tsp (5 mL) lecithin
  OR 1 large egg yolk

1 Tbsp (15 mL) Gelatin Mix
  (see page 185)

1 oz (25 g) white chocolate, melted

4 tsp (20 mL) Vanilla Oil
  (see page 187)

½ cup (125 g) butter, melted

⅓ cup (75 g) cocoa butter, melted

salt and pepper to taste

In a tall and narrow container, blend the grapefruit juice, xanthan gum, and lecithin (if using) with an immersion blender until well combined. Transfer into a saucepan, bring to a boil, and whisk until the mixture starts to thicken. Remove from the heat, add the Gelatin Mix, and stir until dissolved. Combine the chocolate, oil, butter, cocoa butter, and yolk (if using) in a tall and narrow container. Add the hot liquid and immediately blend with an immersion blender until well combined. Season to taste with salt and pepper and keep warm (125°F/60°C) until ready to serve. If you find the mixture is too firm, add more hot grapefruit juice until the mixture reaches the desired consistency.

CRAB | White Chocolate Hollandaise | Potato Brulée | Hot Celery Gelée

For a foamier texture, strain the mixture into a siphon dispenser, add the N$_2$O cartridge, and keep warm (125°F/60°C) in a water bath until ready to serve.

 **version** _____

Omit the cocoa butter and vanilla oil and replace with ½ cup (125 g) butter and replace half of the grapefruit juice with hot whipping cream. Proceed as above.

Assembly

8 Brioche Tuiles (see page 187)

1 pink grapefruit, peeled and segmented

8 celery leaves, or other fresh herbs

sprouts (i.e. onion, garlic, alfalfa)

3 Tbsp (45 mL) finely grated or rasped Parmesan cheese

Preheat the oven to 150°F (65°C). Line 2 baking trays with silicon mats or paper. Cut the Potato Brulée and Hot Celery Gelée into 1 x 2 inch (2.5 x 5 cm) pieces and warm on separate trays in the preheated oven. Heat until evenly warm. Remove both trays from the oven and turn the oven to broil. Lightly dust the tops of the Potato Brulée with freshly grated Parmesan cheese and briefly broil until brown. Place a piece of the Hot Celery Gelée and Potato Brulée onto a warm dish. Arrange the warm Braised Celery Ribs and pink grapefruit segments in a composition of your choice. Finish with a Brioche Tuile, celery leaves, sprouts, and White Chocolate Hollandaise. Serve immediately.

 **assembly**   Omit the Brioche Tuile and replace the Potato Brulée with the e-version Potato Purée instead and proceed as above.

PRAWN | Orange Chili Chocolate Mayonnaise | Wakame Salad | Prawn Meringue
SERVES 8

Prawn Stock

24 prawn shells

1 small onion, chopped

½ stalk celery, chopped

1 clove garlic

3 white button mushrooms

2 star anise

1½ cups (375 mL) water

Combine all the ingredients in a saucepan. Bring to a boil, then simmer for 10 minutes. For faster results use a pressure cooker, bring to pressure, cook for one minute under pressure, remove from the heat source, and let it infuse while the pressure comes down. Strain and store in the refrigerator. Leftovers can be frozen for several months.

Prawn Meringue

⅓ cup (75 mL) Prawn Stock, cold

½ tsp (2.5 mL) xanthan gum

2 Tbsp (30 mL) corn syrup

1 Tbsp (15 mL) Gelatin Mix
  (see page 185)

4 Tbsp (60 mL) egg whites
  (about 2 large)

salt and pepper to taste

Mix the Prawn Stock and xanthan gum until well combined using a high-speed or immersion blender. Transfer the mixture into a saucepan, add the corn syrup, and bring to a boil. At the same time, beat the egg whites to stiff peaks with an electric mixer fitted with a whip attachment. When stiff, pour the hot mixture over the whites while continuing to whip. Add the Gelatin Mix and continue to mix on low speed. Season to taste and serve at once.

Orange Chili Chocolate Mayonnaise

⅓ cup + 2 tsp (85 mL) grapeseed oil

4 cloves garlic, sliced

2 Tbsp (30 mL) freshly squeezed lemon juice

½ cup (125 mL) freshly squeezed orange juice

1 Tbsp (15 mL) corn syrup

2 tsp (10 g) butter

0.7 oz (20 g) white chocolate

1 Tbsp (15 mL) Gelatin Mix (see page 185)

1 tsp (5 mL) Thai chili paste

Heat the grapeseed oil with the garlic in a saucepan. Turn off the heat, cover with a tight fitting lid, and allow it to infuse for a few minutes.

Combine the citrus juices, corn syrup, and butter in another saucepan. Bring to a boil.

Combine the white chocolate, Gelatin Mix, and chili paste in a high speed blender. Pour in the hot juice mixture and garlic oil and blend until well combined. You can store in the refrigerator until ready to use. Serve either warm or cold.

Orange Chili Crumb

1 tsp (5 mL) chili flakes

zest of 1 orange

2 Tbsp (30 mL) toasted sunflower seeds

1 Tbsp (15 mL) bread crumbs

Combine all the ingredients in a small food processor and grind into a powder. Store in a container until needed.

Assembly

3 Tbsp + 1 tsp (50 g) butter

16 prawns, peeled and deveined

salt and pepper to taste

8 dried orange slices (see Fruit Chips, page 188)

2 oranges, peeled and thinly sliced lengthwise

¾ cup (175 mL) prepared wakame salad

3 Tbsp (45 mL) tobiko (flying fish roe)

Melt the butter in a frying pan over low heat. Add the prawns and slowly heat until cooked through. Alternately, cook in a sealed bag in a 150°F (65°C) agitated water bath (see page 36). Season the prawns and place them on a warm serving dish. Spoon or pipe some warm Prawn Meringue onto a plate and arrange the orange segments, prawns, wakame salad, Orange Chili Crumb, dried oranges, and Orange Chili Chocolate Mayonnaise in a composition of your choice. Finish with some tobiko and serve immediately.

e **assembly**   Omit the Prawn Meringue, dried oranges, Orange Chili Crumb and proceed as above.

SHRIMP | Capers Mincemeat Chocolate Jam | Mango Carpaccio | Cucumber Gelée

SERVES 8

Capers Mincemeat Chocolate Jam

6 Tbsp (90 mL) water

2 Tbsp (30 mL) corn syrup

1 tsp (5 mL) Szechuan pepper
(spice used in Asian cooking)

½ vanilla bean, split lengthwise,
seeds removed

2 Tbsp + 2 tsp (40 mL) Gelatin Mix
(see page 185)

⅓ cup (50 g) raisins

2 Tbsp (25 g) capers

1 Tbsp (25 g) prepared mincemeat

2 Tbsp (30 g) butter

1 tsp (5 mL) balsamic vinegar

0.7 oz (20 g) milk chocolate,
coarsely chopped

Bring the water and corn syrup to a
boil. Remove from the heat, add the
Szechuan pepper and vanilla bean.
Cover with a tight-fitting lid and
allow to infuse for 1 hour. Place the
remaining ingredients in a high-speed
blender. Bring the infusion back to a
boil, strain into the blender, and mix
until smooth. Store in the refrigerator.

Cucumber Gelée

1 Tbsp (15 mL) Gelatin Mix
  (see page 185)

6 Tbsp (90 mL) cucumber juice
  (see Vegetable Juice, page 186)

salt and pepper to taste

½ lb (250 g) cooked shrimp
  (90 to 130 count)

Place the Gelatin Mix in a heatproof bowl and briefly melt over a double boiler. Remove from the heat, add the cucumber juice, mix until well combined using a rubber spatula, and season to taste. Add the shrimp, briefly stir, then transfer to a container fitted with a lid. Place in the refrigerator until the mixture is set (it will form a gel). Overnight is best.

Pickled Red Onions

1 medium red onion

2 cups (500 mL) boiling water

4 Tbsp (60 mL) apple cider vinegar

4 Tbsp (60 mL) water

1 Tbsp + 1 tsp (20 mL) honey

¼ tsp (1.25 mL) salt

½ tsp (2.5 mL) peppercorns

Peel and slice the onion as thinly as possible using a sharp knife or mandoline. Place the onion into a bowl, cover with the boiling water, and let it sit for 5 minutes. Drain the water and toss the onions with the remaining ingredients. Let it sit for 10 minutes. Transfer the mixture into a jar with a tight-fitting lid and store in refrigerator for up to 1 week until ready to use.

Assembly

16 to 24 shrimp crackers, uncooked

½ cucumber

1 to 2 fresh mangoes, peeled and thinly sliced

8 strawberry or cherry tomatoes

flesh of 1 fresh young coconut, thinly sliced

8 dried black olives

salt and pepper to taste

Cook the shrimp crackers according to the package instructions. Cut the cucumber in half and remove the seeds. Cut the cucumber halves into 2 inch (5 cm) pieces, then slice into thin strips. Arrange some mango slices, Cucumber Gelée, Pickled Red Onions, cucumber slices, fresh young coconut, olives, and one strawberry tomato in a composition of your choice. Pipe or spoon some Capers Mincemeat Chocolate Jam onto the plate and serve immediately with some shrimp crackers.

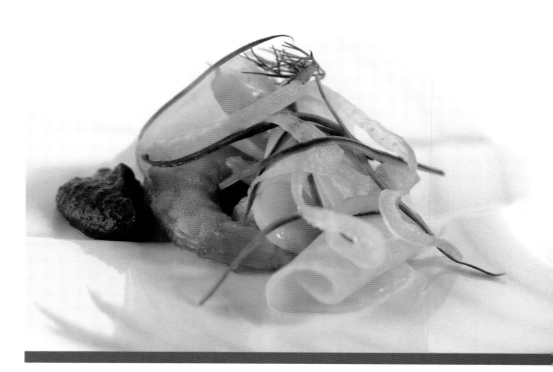

e **assembly**   Omit the shrimp crackers, young coconut, and olives. Proceed as above.

SCALLOP | Baked Grapefruit Chocolate Cheesecake | Asparagus Ribbons | Bacon Porcini Crumble SERVES 8

Baked Grapefruit Chocolate Cheesecake

4 Tbsp (60 mL) grapefruit juice

1.4 oz (40 g) white chocolate, coarsely chopped

¾ cup (175 mL) cream cheese, room temperature

zest of ½ grapefruit

¾ cup (175 mL) sour cream

2 large egg yolks

1½ Tbsp (15 g) all-purpose flour

salt and pepper to taste

Preheat the oven to 300°F (150°C). Place the grapefruit juice and the white chocolate in a small bowl and microwave until the chocolate is melted. Cream the cheese and grapefruit zest with the juice/chocolate mixture using an electric mixer fitted with the paddle attachment. Stop and scrape the bowl with a rubber spatula to ensure thorough mixing. Reduce to the lowest speed, add the sour cream, then bring it up to medium speed until well combined.

Remove the bowl from the machine and add the yolks and flour. Fold by hand using a rubber spatula. Pour the mixture into an 8 inch (20 cm) square pan lined with silicon paper. Bake for 45 minutes in the preheated oven. Turn the pan around and bake for an additional 20 minutes.

Let the cheesecake cool. Cut or break the cheesecake into pieces, place in a food processor, and blend until the mixture is smooth and creamy. Season to taste and keep warm until ready to serve.

Asparagus Ribbons

8 asparagus

2 Tbsp (30 g) butter

salt and pepper to taste

Wash the asparagus and trim the bottoms. Cut into thin strips using a vegetable peeler or mandoline. Microwave the butter until it's very hot. Add the asparagus to the butter and toss. Cook in the microwave in 30-second intervals until the asparagus ribbons are flexible but still crunchy. Season to taste. Note that this recipe should be done as close to serving as possible.

Bacon Porcini Crumble

3 Tbsp (45 mL) water

6 to 8 slices dried Porcini mushrooms (or substitute another dried mushroom)

2 pieces day-old bread

¼ cup (40 g) Caramelized Nuts, chopped (use almonds, see page 185)

4 Tbsp (45 g) icing sugar

3 Tbsp (30 g) cornstarch

4 slices bacon, fried and cut into bits

1 large egg

3 Tbsp (45 g) butter, melted

salt and pepper, to taste

Bring the water to a boil in a ceramic cup in the microwave. Place the cup on the counter, add the dried mushrooms, cover with plastic wrap, and let it sit for at least 15 minutes or until the mushrooms are completely rehydrated.

Squeeze all the water out of the mushrooms, reserving 2 Tbsp (30 mL) of the mushroom liquid. Finely chop the mushrooms and set aside.

Preheat the oven to 250°F (120°C). Cut the bread into ¼ inch (6 mm)

cubes, lay them on a baking tray, and dry for about 15 minutes in the preheated oven. Increase the oven temperature to 325°F (160°C). In a large bowl, combine the bread, almonds, icing sugar, cornstarch, and bacon bits with the chopped mushrooms. Add the egg and melted butter. Mix until evenly coated. Line a baking tray with a silicon mat or paper. Spread the mixture evenly on the tray and bake in the preheated oven until light brown (about 20 minutes). Let it cool, then coarsely chop into a crumble. Store in an airtight container until ready to serve.

Assembly

8 large scallops (or 16 small)

salt and pepper to taste

1 Tbsp (15 g) butter, melted

1 Tbsp (15 mL) grapeseed oil

fish roe (optional)

1 recipe yield Hot Fruit Gelée sheets (use grapefruit, see page 188)

8 grapefruit segments

8 sprigs of fresh dill

Dry the scallops on a paper towel and season to taste with salt and pepper. Heat the butter and oil in a frying pan until very hot. Quickly sear the scallops on both sides (do not overcook). Place 1 or 2 scallops on a warm plate. Pipe or spoon some Baked Grapefruit Chocolate Cheesecake onto the plate. Arrange the Hot Grapefruit Gelée, Asparagus Ribbons, Bacon Porcini Crumble, grapefruit segment, and fish roe (if using) in a composition of your choice. Garnish with some fresh dill and serve immediately.

ℓ assembly Omit the Hot Grapefruit Gelée and fish roe. Use whole asparagus instead of Asparagus Ribbons. Proceed as above.

Sous-vide *is a French term describing the operation of cooking food under vacuum. This method cooks ingredients by heating them for an extended period of time (sometimes over 24 hours), at relatively low temperatures (usually around 140°F/60°C). Because of these parameters, one must be aware of the risk of contamination by botulinum, an anaerobic bacteria that can grow in food in the absence of oxygen at lower temperature. In commercial kitchens, very precise temperature-controlled equipment (thermo-circulators or steam ovens) are used to prevent food safety issues. Although home versions of vacuum machines are readily available and fairly inexpensive, if you don't have one, a simpler alternative is sealed cooking.*

The sealed cooking set-up includes a heatproof vessel filled with water, which is heated by an electric element. The temperature is controlled by a small digital thermometer with a remote probe. Place the food to be cooked in a heavy-duty, self-locking freezer bag (lack of total vacuum will also reduce the risk of botulism contamination). Secure the sealed bag over a dowel across the vessel and agitate the water bath manually (or optionally a relatively inexpensive small air compressor works well also to agitate) from time to time until the food is cooked.

The main advantage of sealed/vacuum cooking is your control of doneness. Meats are done when they reach a specific internal temperature. For example, a meat is rare between 130 to 140°F (55 to 60°C), medium between 140 to 150°F (60 to 65°C), and well done between 150 to 165°F (65 to 75°C). When cooking by conduction (i.e. a frying pan) or radiation (i.e. grill) it is very difficult to evenly cook meat to a specific doneness because of the high heat generated by these methods. Conversely, using the sealed or sous-vide method, the temperature of the water can be accurately controlled to the desired degree of doneness. This process is especially valuable when cooking fish and shellfish because, unlike meats, these proteins are inherently tender and extremely prone to overcooking. Vegetables also benefit from this method, especially roots and tubers.

The sealed environment also prevents the loss of volatile aromatic compounds naturally present in the food and/or added in the bag to scent the main food element (i.e. citrus zest or fresh herbs).

SB¹ | PROCESS | SEALED COOKING

savory
fish | S₂F

SALMON
Cocoa Nib Grapefruit Hot Gelée
Muscovado Tuile | Vanilla Potatoes

TUNA
Spiced Cocoa Rub
Root Ragout | Passion Bonito Ginger Emulsion

MAHI MAHI
Cocoa Oatmeal Granola
Red Swiss Chard | Cumin Crunch

HALIBUT
Cocoa Saffron Butter Emulsion
Tomato Coulis | Horseradish Straws

SALMON | Cocoa Nib Grapefruit Hot Gelée | Muscovado Tuile | Vanilla Potatoes

SERVES 8

Cocoa Muscovado Consommé

1 Tbsp (15 g) muscovado
or demerara sugar

2 tsp (10 mL) corn syrup

½ cup + 1 Tbsp (140 mL) water,
divided

4½ tsp (12 g) cocoa nibs
(see page 202 for resources)

¼ tsp (1.25 mL) anise seeds

½ tsp (2.5 mL) fleur de sel

aged balsamic vinegar to taste

Place the muscovado sugar, corn syrup, and 1 Tbsp (15 mL) of the water into a saucepan over high heat and cook until it reaches a caramel consistency. Remove from the heat and add the remaining ½ cup (125 mL) of water to stop the caramel from cooking further. Add the cocoa nibs, anise seeds, and fleur de sel. Cover with a tight-fitting lid and let it infuse for at least 15 minutes.

Strain the mixture through a fine mesh sieve into a tall and narrow container and discard the solids. Line the sieve with a coffee filter and strain again. Discard the coffee filter with any remaining solids. Add the aged balsamic vinegar and set aside in a sealed container until ready to use.

 version _____

½ cup (125 mL) of the Cocoa
Muscovado Consommé

¼ tsp (1.25 mL) xanthan gum

In a tall and narrow container, blend the Cocoa Muscovado Consommé and xanthan gum with an immersion blender. Transfer into a saucepan and bring the mixture to a boil, whisking continuously. Remove from the heat when the mixture starts to thicken and keep warm until ready to use.

Grapefruit Muscovado Hot Gelée

6 Tbsp (90 mL) freshly squeezed
pink grapefruit juice

6 Tbsp (90 mL) Cocoa Muscovado
Consommé

¾ tsp (3.75 mL) agar powder

4 tsp (20 mL) corn syrup

2 Tbsp + 1 tsp (35 mL) Gelatin Mix
(see page 185)

Line a 10 x 6 inch (25 x 15 cm) pan with a sheet of plastic wrap. In a tall and narrow container, blend the grapefruit juice, Cocoa Muscovado Consommé, and agar with an immersion blender. Transfer into a saucepan and add the corn syrup. Bring the mixture to a boil, whisking continuously. Remove from the heat when the mixture starts to thicken. Add the Gelatin Mix and stir until completely dissolved. Immediately pour it into the plastic-lined pan. Let it set at room temperature.

Vanilla Potatoes

½ cup (125 mL) whipping cream

3 Tbsp (45 mL) milk

1 vanilla bean, seeds scraped

1 tsp (5 mL) salt

½ lb (250 g) Yukon Gold potatoes
(about 3 small), peeled
and quartered

salt and pepper to taste

Bring the cream, milk, and the vanilla
seeds and pod to a boil in a saucepan.
Remove from the heat cover with a
tight-fitting lid. Let it infuse for
15 minutes.

Place the potatoes in a large pot and
cover with cold, salted water. Cook
over medium-high heat until done.
Alternately, use a pressure cooker
and cover the bottom of the cooker
with 2 inches (5 cm) of water; add the
salt and potatoes, bring to pressure,
cook for one minute, then remove from
the heat and let it continue cooking
while the pressure comes down. Drain
the water and pass the potatoes through
a ricer and/or fine mesh sieve until they
are smooth.

Remove the vanilla pod from the
infused cream. Add the infused cream
in batches, while stirring, until the
potatoes are velvety. Season to taste
and keep warm until ready to serve.

Muscovado Tuile

½ tsp (2.5 mL) powdered pectin

1 tsp (5 g) granulated sugar

⅓ cup (75 g) muscovado sugar

3 Tbsp + 1 tsp (50 mL) water

1 Tbsp (15 mL) corn syrup

3 Tbsp + 1 tsp (50 g) softened butter

½ cup (80 g) all-purpose flour

Combine the pectin and both sugars
in a saucepan. Add the water and corn
syrup. Bring to a boil. Remove from
the heat and add the butter. Stir with
a heatproof spatula until the butter
dissolves. Add the flour and mix until
well combined. Transfer the batter into
a container with a lid and store in the
refrigerator until cold.

Preheat the oven to 325°F (160°C).
Line a baking tray with a silicon
mat. Spread the batter onto a sheet
so it's about ⅛ inch (3 mm) thick.
Bake for approximately 5 minutes
in the preheated oven. Let it cool,
break into pieces, then store in an
airtight container.

Assembly

eight 3 oz (75 g) pieces fresh,
skinless salmon

8 segments pink grapefruit

8 sprigs fresh dill

32 edamame beans, cooked

2 Tbsp + 2 tsp (40 mL) salmon roe
(optional)

Fruit Foam (optional, see page 189,
use grapefruit juice)

Preheat the oven to 200°F (95°C).
Line a baking tray with several layers
of moistened cardboard to create an
insulating buffer. Place a silicon mat or
paper on top of the cardboard. Place
the salmon over the silicon mat and
top each one with a piece of Grapefruit
Muscovado Hot Gelée (ensure that
it covers the entire top of each piece
of salmon; it can hang over). Bake for
approximately 15 to 20 minutes in the
preheated oven.

Place a piece of salmon on a warm
plate. Arrange some Vanilla Potatoes,
edamame, grapefruit segments and
salmon roe in a composition of your
choice. Decorate with shards of
Muscovado Tuile and a sprig of dill.
Spoon some Grapefruit Foam onto the
plate, if using and serve immediately.

e assembly Omit the Grapefruit Muscovado Hot Gelée, Grapefruit Foam,
salmon roe and edamame. Instead, serve with the e-version
Cocoa Muscovado Consommé. Proceed as above.

TUNA | Spiced Cocoa Rub | Root Ragout | Passion Bonito Ginger Emulsion

SERVES 8

Spiced Cocoa Rub

3 Tbsp (45 mL) chili powder

1 Tbsp (15 mL) cocoa powder

1½ tsp (7.5 mL) finely ground
   black pepper

eight 3 oz (75 g) pieces ahi tuna

oil for pan-frying

Combine the chili powder, cocoa, and pepper in a bowl. Thoroughly dry the surface of the tuna with a paper towel. Dredge the tuna slices in the rub. Heat the oil in a frying pan until very hot. Sear the tuna on each side until cooked as desired. Keep warm.

Root Ragout

8 parsnips, peeled

4 small yellow beets

16 baby carrots

4 Tbsp (60 mL) olive oil

salt and pepper to taste

Preheat the oven to 325°F (160°C). Combine all the vegetables in a small bowl and toss with the olive oil. Season to taste and place on a baking tray. Put the tray in the preheated oven and cook until the vegetables are tender.

Sesame Peas Crumb

¼ cup (28 g) roasted green peas
   (available in Asian specialty
   food stores)

1 Tbsp (15 mL) toasted sesame seeds

Grind the above ingredients into a fine powder using a food processor. Store in an airtight container.

Passion Fruit Bonito Ginger Emulsion

4 Tbsp (60 mL) water

6 Tbsp (90 mL) Fruit Purée (use
   passion fruit, see page 186)

1 oz (25 g) fresh ginger, peeled

2 Tbsp (30 mL) bonito flakes

6 Tbsp (90 mL)
   grapeseed oil

2 tsp (10 g) butter

0.7 oz (20 g) white chocolate

1 Tbsp (15 mL) Gelatin Mix
   (see page 185)

1 Tbsp (15 mL) corn syrup

Bring the water, passion fruit purée, and ginger to a boil in a saucepan. Remove from the heat, add the bonito flakes, cover with a tight fitting lid, and let it infuse for at least 30 minutes.

Heat the oil, butter, and white chocolate in the microwave or over a double boiler. Strain the passion fruit juice infusion through a sieve, discard the remnants, and heat the infusion back to about 125°F (60°C). Add the Gelatin Mix and corn syrup to the passion fruit juice infusion and stir until dissolved. Combine the chocolate and infusion mixtures in a blender and whirl on high until smooth. Store in the refrigerator until ready to use. Serve warm.

Assembly

1 oz (25 g) pea shoots

16 Roasted Onions (see page 190)

Arrange the Spiced Cocoa Rub, ahi tuna, Root Ragout, Roasted Onions, Sesame Peas Crumb, and Passion Fruit Bonito Ginger Emulsion in a composition of your choice. Garnish with some pea shoots and serve immediately.

assembly   Omit the Sesame Peas Crumb.
Proceed as above.

MAHI MAHI | Cocoa Oatmeal Granola | Red Swiss Chard | Cumin Crunch

SERVES 8

Cocoa Oatmeal Granola

1 Tbsp (15 mL) honey

½ tsp (2.5 mL) truffle oil

2 Tbsp (30 g) butter, melted

½ cup (50 g) rolled oats

2 Tbsp (20 g) shredded
   unsweetened coconut

pinch salt

⅓ cup (60 g) brown sugar

½ tsp (2.5 mL) cumin seeds

¾ tsp (3.75 mL) unsweetened
   cocoa powder

Preheat the oven to 350°F (180°C).
Combine the honey, truffle oil, and
butter in a bowl. Mix well. Add the
rest of the ingredients and blend with a
rubber spatula until well combined. Line
a baking tray with a silicon mat or paper.
Place the granola onto the baking tray
and bake for approximately 25 minutes
in the preheated oven. Let it cool, then
store in an airtight container.

Red Swiss Chard

8 stalks red Swiss chard (with leaves)

2 Tbsp (30 mL) olive oil

salt and pepper to taste

2 Tbsp (30 g) butter

1 tsp (5 mL) fresh ginger,
    peeled and finely chopped

Clean and trim the Swiss chard.
Separate the stalks from the leaves.
Set the leaves aside and thinly slice
the stalks. Heat the oil in a saucepan
and cook the stalks until crispy.
Season to taste.

Heat the butter and ginger in a
saucepan and cook the chard leaves
until just wilted. Season to taste.
Keep the stalks and leaves warm
until ready to serve.

 version _____

Leave the stalks whole and cook in the
butter and ginger first, then add the
leaves. Season to taste and keep warm
until ready to serve.

Cumin Crunch

⅓ cup (60 g) demerara sugar

½ tsp (2.5 mL) unsweetened
    cocoa powder

1½ tsp (7.5 mL) cumin seeds

½ tsp (2.5 mL) fleur de sel

Preheat the oven to 350°F (180°C).
Mix all the ingredients together
in bowl.

Line a baking tray with a silicon mat
and divide the mixture into 8 to 10
portions. Evenly sprinkle 2 separate
portions of the mixture onto the silicon
mat (leave enough space between
so that when they melt they do not
touch). Place another silicon mat on

top and bake for approximately 10
minutes in the preheated oven. Remove
from the oven and peel off the top
silicon mat. While the sugar is still
warm, stretch it into shapes of your
choice. Repeat with the remaining
mixture. Once the shapes are cooled,
store them in an airtight container.

Assembly

eight 3 oz (75 g) pieces mahi mahi

2 Tbsp (30 mL) olive oil

enoki mushrooms

watermelon radish, thinly sliced

8 to 24 edible flowers (optional)

Thoroughly dry the surface of the
mahi mahi with a paper towel. Heat
the oil in a frying pan until very hot.
Sear the mahi mahi on both sides until
cooked as desired.

Toss the Swiss chard stalks and
enoki mushrooms together in a
bowl. Arrange the mahi mahi, Cocoa
Oatmeal Granola, wilted chard leaves,
watermelon radish and Swiss chard
stalk/enoki mushroom mixture in a
composition of your choice. Garnish
with the Cumin Crunch and edible
flowers (if using). Serve immediately.

assembly Omit the Cumin Crunch, watermelon radish and enoki
mushrooms. Instead, serve with the e-version Red Swiss Chard.
Proceed as above.

HALIBUT | Cocoa Saffron Butter Emulsion | Tomato Coulis | Horseradish Straws

SERVES 8

Braised Green Onions

16 green onions, washed
    and trimmed

2 slices smoked bacon, cooked
    and chopped

2 Tbsp (30 mL) olive oil

2 Tbsp (30 mL) white wine

½ cup (125 mL) Vegetable Stock
    (see page 190)

3 sprigs fresh thyme

salt and pepper to taste

Wash the green onions and cut away
most of the greens, setting them aside
for the poaching liquid.

Place all of the ingredients in a sealed
bag, season to taste, and cook in a
150°F (65°C) agitated water bath
(see page 36) for approximately 45
minutes or until done. Alternately,
cook in a small, covered pot over low
heat until the onions are soft but still
maintain their shape. Keep warm until
ready to serve.

Tomato Coulis

8 Roma tomatoes, halved and seeded

4 Tbsp (60 mL) extra virgin olive oil

kosher salt and freshly ground black
    pepper to taste

1 bunch fresh thyme

½ tsp (2.5 mL) Gelatin Mix
    (see page 185)

0.4 oz (10 g) milk chocolate

balsamic vinegar to taste

Preheat the oven to 250°F (120°C).
Line a baking tray with a silicon mat
and place all of the tomato halves
(cavity up) on top. Drizzle with olive
oil and sprinkle with the salt and
pepper, and thyme leaves. Bake for
1½ to 2 hours in the preheated oven
(the tomatoes should be semi-dried).

Place the warm tomatoes and oil from the pan in a food processor. Add the Gelatin Mix and milk chocolate and blend until the mixture reaches the consistency of ketchup. Check for seasoning and add some balsamic vinegar to taste. Store in a sealed container in the refrigerator for up to 1 week. Serve warm.

Cocoa Saffron Butter Emulsion

¼ cup + 1 tsp (65 mL) whipping cream

1 pinch Spanish saffron

4 Tbsp (60 mL) cocoa butter, melted

2 Tbsp (30 mL) extra virgin olive oil

2 Tbsp (30 mL) white wine

salt to taste

1 tsp (5 mL) Gelatin Mix (see page 185)

Bring the whipping cream to a boil over high heat. Add the saffron, remove from the heat, cover with a tight-fitting lid, and let it infuse for at least 20 minutes.

Add the remaining ingredients, except the Gelatin Mix. Place over high heat until the mixture is almost boiling. Pour the mixture into a tall and narrow container, add the Gelatin Mix, stir until dissolved, and keep warm. Right before serving, blend with an immersion blender until the mixture is frothy.

Horseradish Straws

½ cup (125 mL) milk

3 Tbsp + 1 tsp (50 g) butter

pinch salt

⅔ cup + 2 Tbsp (125 g) all-purpose flour

2 large eggs

2 tsp (10 mL) chives, finely chopped

2 tsp (10 mL) prepared horseradish

Preheat the oven to 350°F (180°C). Heat the milk, butter, and salt in a saucepan over medium heat until the butter is melted. Bring to a boil. Remove from the heat, add the flour, and mix with a wooden spoon until well incorporated. Return the saucepan to medium heat for about 1 minute, stirring constantly to 'dry' the mixture. Remove from the heat and add the eggs, one at a time (ensure the first egg is well incorporated before adding the second). Add the chives and horseradish. Mix until well incorporated.

Line a baking tray with a silicon mat. Using a piping bag, pipe long, thin lines of the mixture onto the baking tray (leave space between each line so they don't stick together). Bake in the preheated oven until golden brown (about 5 minutes). Let them cool, then store in an airtight container. This recipe makes more than required and leftovers can be stored frozen for several weeks.

Poaching Liquid

1 cup (250 mL) white wine

3 cups (750 mL) Vegetable Stock (see page 190) or water

1 Tbsp (15 mL) black peppercorns

4 sprigs lemon thyme

tops of 16 green onions

salt to taste

Place all the ingredients in the saucepan and cook, covered for 10 minutes on medium heat. Alternately, place all the ingredients in a pressure cooker, bring to pressure, cook for one minute under pressure, remove from heat source and let infuse/cook while the pressure comes down on its own. After either method of cooking, strain the mixture and discard solids and store in the refrigerator for up to 1 week or several weeks in the freezer.

HALIBUT | Cocoa Saffron Butter Emulsion | Tomato Coulis | Horseradish Straws

Assembly

eight 3 oz (90 g) pieces halibut, skin removed

4 oz (110 g) package shimeji mushrooms (other mushrooms may be substituted)

oil for sautéing

salt and pepper to taste

8 Broiled Tomatoes, use yellow tomatoes (see page 190)

1 recipe yield Mushroom Emulsion (see page 190)

8 lemon thyme sprigs

Bring the Poaching Liquid to a boil, remove from the heat and add the pieces of halibut. Let the fish stand in the hot liquid for about 4 minutes or until the fish is just done. If not thoroughly cooked, remove the halibut, bring the poaching liquid back to a boil, remove from the heat source, place the halibut back into the hot liquid, and let it stand until desired doneness. Briefly sauté the shimeji mushrooms in some oil and season with salt and pepper.

Place a piece of halibut on a warm plate. Pipe or spoon some Tomato Coulis and Mushroom Emulsion onto the plate and arrange some of the Braised Green Onions, sautéed shimeji mushrooms, and Broiled Tomatoes in a composition of your choice. Decorate with some lemon thyme and Horseradish Straws. Spoon some frothed Cocoa Saffron Butter Emulsion. Serve immediately.

ⓔ assembly   Omit the Horseradish Straws, Broiled Tomatoes, and Mushroom Emulsion. Proceed as above.

Although gelatin is the major hydrocolloid used for gelling, other hydrocolloids are becoming increasingly common in modern Western cuisine, particularly agar. Agar is a polysaccharide (galactose sugar) obtained from red seaweed (Rhodophycae). The word agar comes from the Malay word "agar-agar," meaning jelly. Agar is insoluble in cold water but following heating to the boiling point and subsequent cooling, the long molecules of agar start to lose energy and line up to form a network, gelling up to 99.5% of the liquid within. Agar forms clear, stable, and firm gels that remain solid up to temperatures of about 180°F (80°C). Agar has similar applications as gelatin, but unlike gelatin, it allows gels to be made hot and served hot. This unique property provides opportunities to make preparations with modern tastes and/or textures such as hot infusion gelées or vegetable brulée.

The typical ratio to make an agar gel is around 1% of total liquids. However, the least amount of agar is best as too much will result in a gel with a grainy texture. Agar gels are not very elastic and actually break quite easily and thus, these gels are best served flat or cut into small shapes. Elasticity can be improved through the addition of some sorbitol or glycerin.

Salt, sugar, or slight acidity does not affect the gelling process with agar. However, since liquids need to be heated to the boiling point, for fresh herb juices and other similar liquids that are prone to quick oxidation, agar is not recommended as the gelling agent. Other specialty hydrocolloids yielding similar gelling properties as agar are starting to surface, such as carageenan and gellan. These provide increased elasticity, softer setting, and/or a lower melting point. Since all of these hydrocolloids are plant based, they can also be used as a vegetarian alternative to gelatin.

SB² | TEXTURE | AGAR

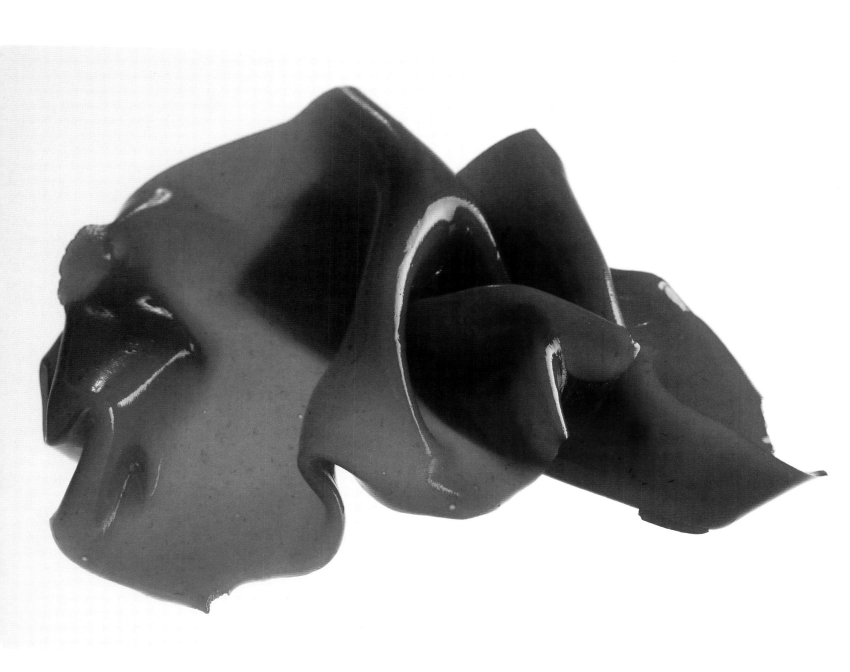

savory
meat | S$_3$M

BEEF
ChocoWine Gelée Pavé
Cauliflower Emulsion | Filo Crisp

LAMB
Chocolate Merlot Blueberry Jam
Apple Pasta | Cumin Yogurt Cheese

PORK
Date Carrot Chocolate Confit
Crispy Gnocchi | Mole Paper

DUCK
Chocolate Port Reduction
Spiced Almond Crumb | Stewed Cherries

BEEF | ChocoWine Gelée Pavé | Cauliflower Emulsion | Filo Crisp

SERVES 8

Braised Short Ribs

2 carrots

2 stalks celery

1 onion

½ small leek

2 cloves garlic

2 to 3 Tbsp (30 to 45 mL) olive oil

8 to 16 beef short ribs

1 bay leaf

3 sprigs fresh thyme

3 sprigs fresh parsley
  (stalk and leaves)

1 small sprig fresh rosemary

½ cup (125 mL) red wine

water (enough to cover
  all ingredients)

salt and pepper to taste

3.6 oz (100 g) 70% dark chocolate
  (e-version only)

Peel, clean, and coarsely chop the carrots, celery, onion, leek, and garlic. Place into a large bowl and set aside.

Add the oil to an ovenproof pan or skillet over medium-high heat. Cook the short ribs on each side until the meat has reached a caramelized brown color. Remove the meat from pan and set aside.

Preheat the oven to 300°F (150°C). Add the reserved, chopped vegetables to the pan and cook for approximately 1 minute. Add the bay leaf, thyme, parsley, and rosemary. Place the meat over the vegetables and add the red wine. Add cold water until all the ingredients are just covered. Season to taste. Place a tight-fitting lid over the pan, or cover with aluminum foil, and braise in the preheated oven for approximately 3 hours or until the meat easily pulls apart.

Remove the meat from the braising liquid. Separate the meat from the bones and discard the bones. Keep the meat warm and set aside.

Strain the braising liquid using a fine sieve or cheesecloth (don't press the vegetables, as the flesh will turn the braising liquid cloudy). Discard the vegetables and herbs. Let the liquid settle for a few minutes so that any sediment has a chance to sink to the bottom and any excess fat can rise to the top. Skim off the fat and discard. Slowly transfer the liquid into another container, making sure not to disturb or include any of the sediment. Set aside.

e version _____

Measure 1½ cups (375 mL) of the clear braising liquid and reduce in a saucepan by half.
Place the chocolate in a tall and narrow container, add the boiling braising liquid, and emulsify using an immersion blender until well combined. Keep warm.

ChocoWine Gelée Pavé

Reserved Braised Short Ribs meat (warm)

4 Tbsp (60 mL) red wine

¾ cup + 2 tsp (185 mL) reserved braising liquid

1 tsp (5 mL) chili powder or to taste

1 tsp 5 mL) agar powder

1½ tsp (7 mL) Gelatin Mix (see page 185)

1.9 oz (50 g) 70% dark chocolate, finely chopped

Line an 8 inch (20 cm) square pan with a sheet of plastic wrap. Place the Braised Short Ribs meat at the bottom and press to make sure the top is evenly flat. Combine the red wine, braising liquid, and agar powder in a tall and narrow container. Blend with an immersion blender. Transfer the mixture into a saucepan and bring to a boil while continuously whisking. As soon as the mixture begins to thicken, remove from the heat, add the Gelatin Mix, whisk in the dark chocolate, and mix until well combined. Immediately pour over the warm meat. Let this set at room temperature, then transfer to the refrigerator. Once cooled, cut the Pavé into 8 pieces. Before serving, reheat the cut Pavé in a 225°F (105°C) oven until warm.

Cauliflower Emulsion

2 slices white bread

1 clove garlic, chopped

3 Tbsp (45 mL) olive oil

4 Tbsp (60 mL) whipping cream

1 cup (160 g) cauliflower florets, steamed

Remove the crust of the bread and cut into small cubes. Place in a bowl.

Briefly cook the garlic and oil in a saucepan over medium heat, then pour on top of the bread.

Bring the whipping cream to a boil, remove from the heat, and add to the bread. Stir until the bread is completely coated with the cream.

Purée the cauliflower in a food processor, add the bread mixture and lemon juice and continue blending until the mixture is smooth. Season to taste. Optionally, pass the mixture through a fine mesh strainer. Keep warm.

Filo Crisp

4½ oz (115 g) filo dough

¼ cup (60 g) butter, melted

Preheat the oven to 350°F (180°C). Cut the dough into thin strips. Line a baking tray with a silicon mat or paper and shape the strips into eight 2 inch (5 cm) circles. Liberally brush the melted butter over the filo circles and bake in the preheated oven until golden brown (about 10 minutes). Keep warm.

Assembly

3 Tbsp (45 mL) olive oil, for frying

8 cauliflower florets, cut in half

salt and pepper to taste

Mushroom Emulsion (see page 190)

16 Roasted Shallots (see page 190)

8 morels (optional)

Herb Oil (use parsley, see page 187)

8 sprigs flat leaf parsley

red chili peppers (optional)

Preheat the oven to 350° (180°C). Heat the oil in a heatproof pan or skillet. Place the cauliflower florets flat side down and cook until golden brown. Turn over, season to taste and finish cooking in the preheated oven until soft, but still holding their shape.

Pipe or spoon some Mushroom Emulsion and Cauliflower Emulsion onto a warm plate. Arrange a piece of ChocoWine Gelée Pavé, Roasted Shallots, roasted cauliflower, and a morel mushroom briefly sautéed in butter (if using) in a composition of your choice. Finish with the Filo Crisp, parsley oil, a sprig of parsley, and a few pieces of red chili (if using). Serve immediately.

ℯ assembly   Omit the ChocoWine Gelée Pavé. Arrange the Braised Short Ribs, emulsified ChocoWine Sauce, Cauliflower Emulsion, and Roasted Shallots in a composition of your choice. Finish with the Filo Crisp and a sprig of parsley. Serve immediately.

LAMB | Chocolate Merlot Blueberry Jam | Apple Pasta | Cumin Yogurt Cheese

SERVES 8

Chocolate Merlot Blueberry Jam

⅓ cup (75 mL) red wine

⅓ cup (65 g) dried blueberries

0.6 oz (15 g) 70% dark chocolate, finely chopped

2 Tbsp (30 g) butter

Combine the wine and dried blueberries in a container and warm in the microwave. Place the dark chocolate and butter in a high-speed blender, add the hot wine mixture and blitz until smooth. Keep warm until ready to serve.

Lamb Tenderloin

2 Tbsp (30 g) butter

2 Tbsp (30 mL) olive oil

1 lb (500 g) lamb tenderloin

Heat the butter and olive oil in a frying pan over high heat. Add the lamb and cook until desired doneness (note that lamb is best served rare to medium rare). Remove from the heat and let the meat rest for a few minutes, then cut 8 servings from the tenderloin.

Apple Pasta

2 cups (500 mL) cold water

1 tsp (5 mL) ascorbic acid OR
    2 Tbsp (30 mL) freshly squeezed
    lemon juice

2 to 3 apples

Prepare a bowl with the water, acidulated with some lemon juice or ascorbic acid. To make fruit sheets, a vegetable slicer is required. However, if you don't have such a machine, you can slice the apple using a very sharp knife or mandoline. As soon as they are cut, plunge the apple slices into the water. Do this step as close to serving as possible.

Cumin Yogurt Cheese

1 cup (250 mL) plain yogurt
    (select a yogurt that does not
    contain any gelatin)

1 Tbsp (15 mL) olive oil

2 tsp (10 mL) cumin seeds

Line a sieve with a coffee filter, then place the sieve over a container (leave at least 1½ inches/4 cm between the sieve and the bottom of the container). Spoon the yogurt into the filter and let it sit overnight in the refrigerator. After draining, you should have ½ cup (125 mL) of yogurt cheese in the filter. Transfer this cheese to a bowl and discard the drained liquid.

Toast the oil and cumin seeds in a saucepan over medium heat. Add to the yogurt cheese and mix until well combined. Place the mixture in a sealed container and refrigerate for at least 2 hours (overnight is best).

Pancetta Shards

16 pieces pancetta

Preheat the oven to 375°F (190°C). Lay the pancetta slices on a baking tray lined with silicon paper. If all of the pancetta does not fit on the first layer, place another piece of silicon paper on top and repeat. Bake until all the fat has melted, remove the silicon paper and continue baking until the pancetta is crispy. (Note: you may have to flip the pancetta to crisp both sides.) Break the pancetta into shards.

Assembly

16 Broiled Tomatoes, use grape
    tomatoes (see page 190)

fresh rosemary

16 pieces Lemon Confit
    (optional, see page 188)

Pipe or spoon some Chocolate Merlot Blueberry Jam onto a warm plate. Arrange the Lamb Tenderloin, Apple Pasta, Cumin Yogurt Cheese, and Broiled Tomatoes in a composition of your choice. Finish with some Pancetta Shards, fresh rosemary, and Lemon Confit (if using). Serve immediately.

ℯ assembly   Omit the Apple Pasta and Lemon Confit. Proceed as above.

PORK | Date Carrot Chocolate Confit | Crispy Gnocchi | Mole Paper

SERVES 8

Pulled Pork

4 Tbsp (60 mL) olive oil

one 1½ lb (750 g) pork shoulder

1 large carrot

1 small onion

1 clove garlic

2 star anise

1 small cinnamon stick

1 tsp (5 mL) fennel seeds

½ tsp (2.5 mL) black peppercorns

4 Tbsp (60 mL) white wine

2 Tbsp (30 mL) barbecue sauce

water

salt to taste

Preheat the oven to 300°F (150°C). Heat the oil over high heat in an ovenproof skillet and sear the pork on all sides. Remove the meat, add the carrot, onion, garlic, star anise, cinnamon, fennel, and peppercorns. Sauté for 1 to 2 minutes. Place the seared pork over the vegetables, add the wine and barbecue sauce, and top with enough water to cover about ⅔ of the contents. Season to taste. Place a tight fitting lid over the skillet, or cover with aluminum foil, and braise in the preheated oven until the meat easily pulls apart (about 2½ hours). Alternately, use a pressure cooker and cook the above under pressure for approximately 40 minutes. Let the pressure come down on its own, remove the pork, pull the meat apart, and keep warm.

Date Carrot Chocolate Confit

4 Tbsp (60 mL) carrot juice
(see Vegetable Juice, page 186)

8 dried dates, chopped

2 Tbsp (30 mL) hoisin sauce

1 tsp (5 mL) freshly grated ginger

2 tsp (10 mL) freshly squeezed
lemon juice

1.1 oz (30 g) milk chocolate, melted

Heat the carrot juice and dates in a microwaveable container. Cover with a lid or plastic wrap and let it sit until the dates are soft (about 10 minutes). Reheat the date mixture, transfer to a food processor, and blend to a smooth paste. Add the rest of the ingredients and continue blending until smooth. Either keep warm until ready to serve, or refrigerate and reheat before serving. Keeps in the refrigerator for up to 1 week.

Crispy Gnocchi

8 oz (225 g) gnocchi (about 48 pieces)

3 Tbsp (45 g) butter

3 Tbsp (45 mL) olive oil

3 Tbsp (20 g) roasted cocoa nibs (see page 202 for resources)

Chinese five spice powder to taste

Cook the gnocchi according to the package instructions. Once cooked, drain and place on a paper towel to drain any excess water. Keep warm.

Cook the butter to the Brown Butter stage (see page 188). Add the oil, cocoa nibs, Chinese five spice powder, and cooked gnocchi. Toss until the gnocchi are brown and crispy. Season to taste and keep warm.

Mole Paper

eight 3 inch (8 cm) square wonton wrapper sheets

1 tsp (5 mL) chili powder

1 tsp (5 mL) unsweetened cocoa powder

3 Tbsp (45 g) butter, melted

0.6 oz (15 g) dark chocolate, melted

Preheat the oven to 350°F (180°C). Place the wonton wrappers on a baking sheet. In a small bowl, mix all the remaining ingredients with a spatula until well combined. Brush this mixture onto each sheet of wonton dough. Place the baking tray in the preheated oven and bake the wontons until crispy (3 to 5 minutes). Once cooled, break into shards and store in an airtight container.

Assembly

½ fresh pineapple, peeled, cored, and quartered

1 recipe yield Hot Fruit Gelée sheets (use pineapple, see page 188)

8 to 16 baby bok choy

butter for sautéing

salt and pepper to taste

8 fresh carrot slices, steamed

8 sprigs fresh herbs (thyme, parsley, etc.)

Preheat the oven to 350°F (180°C). Line a baking tray with a silicon mat or paper. Cut the pineapple into ½ inch (1 cm) thick slices. Place on the baking tray and roast in the preheated oven until some of the natural sugar starts to caramelize (about 20 minutes). Reduce the oven temperature to 225°F (105°C) and keep warm.

Cut the Hot Pineapple Gelée sheets into 4 inch (10 cm) squares. Place some warm Pulled Pork along one edge of the square and roll into a cylinder. Line a baking tray with a silicon mat or paper. Place the Gelée cylinders onto the baking tray and warm in the preheated oven.

Briefly sauté the baby bok choy with some butter and season to taste.

Pipe or spoon some Date Carrot Chocolate Confit onto a warm plate. Arrange a Pineapple Pork cylinder, Crispy Gnocchi, caramelized pineapple, baby bok choy, and a steamed carrot slice in a composition of your choice. Finish with some shards of Mole Paper and fresh herb leaves. Serve immediately.

assembly   Omit the Hot Pineapple Gelée, Carrot Slices, Baby Bok Choy. Serve the Pulled Pork as is. Proceed as above.

DUCK | Chocolate Port Reduction | Spiced Almond Crumb | Stewed Cherries

SERVES 8

Chocolate Port Reduction

1 small onion, finely chopped

1 clove garlic, finely chopped

1 small dried ancho chili

1 Tbsp (15 mL) olive oil

3 Tbsp (45 mL) red wine

Stewed Cherries liquid

0.9 oz (25 g) 70% dark chocolate, finely chopped

Sauté the onion, garlic, ancho chili, and olive oil in a saucepan over low heat until the onions are translucent. Add the red wine and Stewed Cherries liquid and continue cooking until the mixture reduces by half.

Place the chocolate into a tall and narrow container, strain the hot liquid through a cheesecloth into the chocolate, and blend with an immersion blender until well combined. If needed, return the mixture to the saucepan and continue reducing over low heat, while continuously stirring, until the desired consistency is reached.

Stewed Cherries

16 dried cherries, halved

1 cup (250 mL) port

2 tsp (10 g) butter, melted

freshly ground pepper to taste

Place the dried cherries in a container fitted with a lid. Heat the port until it nearly boils, then pour on top of the cherries and seal the container immediately. Let this sit for at least 3 hours (overnight is best). Strain the liquid from the cherries and reserve for the Chocolate Port Reduction. Just before serving, briefly warm the cherries in a saucepan with the butter. Season with freshly ground pepper.

Butternut Squash Terrine

one 1 lb (500 g) butternut squash

1 Tbsp (15 g) butter, melted

1 Tbsp (15 mL) olive oil

1 Tbsp (15 mL) honey

½ cup (125 mL) water

zest and freshly squeezed juice
of 1 orange

¼ tsp (1.25 mL) Chinese five spice
powder

1 tsp (5 mL) agar powder

1½ tsp (7.5 mL) Gelatin Mix
(see page 185)

salt and pepper to taste

Preheat the oven to 350°F (180° C). Peel the squash and remove the seeds. Cut the squash into ¼ inch (6 mm) slices. Line an 8 inch (20 cm) baking dish or pan with silicon paper. Fill the dish with the squash slices and season to taste. Combine all the remaining ingredients in a saucepan, except for the agar powder, Gelatin Mix, and salt and pepper. Place the saucepan over high heat until the mixture almost reaches a boil, then pour over the squash. Cover the baking pan with a sheet of aluminum foil and bake in the preheated oven for 20 to 30 minutes. Let it cool and drain all of the liquid into a tall and narrow container. Add the agar to the liquid and immediately blend with an immersion blender. Transfer to a saucepan, bring to a boil, and whisk until the mixture begins to thicken. Remove from the heat, add the Gelatin Mix, stir until dissolved, and immediately pour over the squash. Let it cool, then transfer the baking tray to the refrigerator to set completely. Before serving, cut the set squash into desired shapes and reheat in a 225°F (105°C) oven.

℮ version

Omit the agar/Gelatin Mix step and as soon as the squash is baked, mash it into a smooth purée, season to taste, and keep warm.

Spiced Almond Crumb

½ recipe yield Caramelized Nuts,
use almonds (see page 185)

¼ tsp (1.25 mL) Chinese five spice
powder

Grind the Caramelized Nuts with the Chinese five spice powder in a food processor. Store in an airtight container.

Honey Pepper Glass

2 Tbsp (30 mL) honey

⅓ cup (75 mL) corn syrup

1 tsp (5 mL) freshly ground
black pepper

Preheat the oven to 350°F (180°C). Line a baking tray with a silicon mat. Mix all the ingredients together in a small bowl and warm in the microwave for about 20 to 30 seconds. Dip a 3 inch (8 cm) brush into the mixture, and paint rectangular outlines (about 5 inches/ 12 cm wide). Bake for 5 minutes in the preheated oven. Allow the strips to cool for about 30 seconds, then stretch into desired shapes. Let it cool completely, and store in an airtight container.

Assembly

4 duck breasts (you can substitute
chicken breasts)

3 Tbsp (45 mL) olive oil

salt and pepper to taste

8 broccolini, steamed

salt and pepper to taste

Score the duck's skin to render as much fat as possible. Heat the oil in a frying pan over high heat. Place the duck breasts in the pan, skin side down, and cook until brown and crispy. Flip the breasts and season the skin. Reduce the heat to medium-low and continue cooking until desired doneness. Let the breasts rest for a few minutes, then slice.

Pipe or spoon some Chocolate Port Reduction onto a warm plate. Arrange one or more pieces of duck, some Stewed Cherries, warm Butternut Squash Terrine, and steamed broccolini in a composition of your choice. Finish with some Spiced Almond Crumb and a piece of Honey Pepper Glass. Serve immediately.

 assembly   Omit the Honey Pepper Glass and Spiced Almond Crumb.
Use the Butternut Squash Terrine e-version. Proceed as above.

Change means to continually question and not take tradition for granted:
creativity comes best when one seeks and changes often.

2006 SOUTH BEACH WINE & FOOD FESTIVAL:
CINNAMON, DRIED CHERRIES & PLUMS

sweet
herbal | S₁H

BASIL
Chocolate Lemon Cream
Almond Basil Cake | Raspberry Water Gelée

MINT
Chocolate Cheese Mousse
Hot Orange Carrot Gelée | Fig Mint Confit

ROSE
Chocolate Mango Custard
Rose Lychee Meringue | Coconut Crumble

TARRAGON
Chocolate Vanilla Pudding
Caramelized Puffed Rice | Tarragon Emulsion

BASIL | Chocolate Lemon Cream | Almond Basil Cake | Raspberry Water Gelée

SERVES 8

Vanilla Cream Leather

1 cup + 3 Tbsp (300 g) Pastry Cream
(see page 186)

1 vanilla bean, seeds scraped

Preheat the oven to 200°F (95°C).
While the Pastry Cream is still hot,
add the vanilla seeds and mix until
well combined.

Line a tray with a silicon mat. Using
an offset spatula, spread the hot
Pastry Cream into a thin and even
layer. Bake in the preheated oven for

approximately 30 minutes. Peel the
layer of Pastry Cream from the silicon
mat, flip, and continue baking until
dry (another 5 to 10 minutes). Cut the
Leather into 3 x 10.5 inch (8 x 26 cm)
pieces and set aside.

Almond and Basil Oil Cake

4 large egg yolks

1 Tbsp (15 mL) Herb Oil (use basil,
see page 187)

⅓ cup + 1 Tbsp (80 g) granulated
sugar, divided

1⅔ cup (180 g) finely ground
almonds

1 Tbsp + 1 tsp (12 g) all-purpose flour

2 tsp (10 mL) baking powder

4 large egg whites

Preheat the oven to 350°F (180°C).
Whisk the egg yolks and Herb Oil
with 3 Tbsp (45g) of the sugar until
light and fluffy. Add the almonds, flour,
and baking powder and fold into the
yolk mixture using a rubber spatula.

Whip the egg whites using an electric
mixer fitted with a whisk attachment.
When the whites no longer gain
volume and start to slide from the sides
of the bowl, add the remaining sugar
and continue whipping until it forms
stiff peaks.

Mix ⅓ of the whites into the yolk mixture, then add the rest of the whites and gently fold using a rubber spatula.

Line a 6 x 8 inch (15 x 20 cm) baking tray with a silicon mat or paper. Evenly spread the batter and bake for 20 to 25 minutes. Cut the cake into 3 x 1 x 1 inch (7.5 x 2.5 x 2.5 cm) square tubes. Cover with plastic wrap and set aside. This cake will store in the freezer for several weeks.

Chocolate Lemon Cream

4 Tbsp (60 mL) sour cream

zest of ½ lemon

4.3 oz (120 g) white chocolate, melted

Warm the sour cream over a double boiler or in the microwave. Add the lemon zest and melted chocolate and whisk until well combined. Place the mixture in a sealed container and let it set in the refrigerator.

Raspberry Water Gelée

1 Tbsp + 1 tsp (20 mL) Gelatin Mix (see page 185)

¾ cup + 1 Tbsp (190 mL) Fruit Water (use raspberries, see page 190)

2 tsp (10 mL) honey

2 tsp (10 mL) Amaretto (optional)

Place the Gelatin Mix in a heatproof bowl and briefly melt over a double boiler. Remove from the heat, add the remaining ingredients and mix using a rubber spatula until well combined. Transfer the mixture to a container with a tight-fitting lid and let it set at room temperature.

Assembly

1 cup (250 mL) milk, warm

Herb Emulsion (use basil, see page 188)

16 to 24 Chocolate Puff Pastry sticks (see page 189)

1 cup (250 mL) Fruit Foam (use raspberry water, see page 189)

basil leaves (optional)

assembly   8 small glasses, warm

Omit the Basil Emulsion, Chocolate Puff Pastry, and Raspberry Foam.

Double the Raspberry Water Gelée recipe and heat it over a double boiler or in the microwave. Transfer to a tall and narrow container and blend with an immersion blender until it becomes frothy. Pour the mixture into the warm glasses and let it sit for about 1 minute or until it separates into a liquid and foam.

Soak the Vanilla Cream Leather pieces in warm milk until soft. Place a few pieces of Vanilla Cream Leather on top of a piece of Almond and Basil Oil Cake and serve with some Chocolate Lemon Cream on the side. Serve immediately.

Soak the Vanilla Cream Leather pieces in the warm milk until soft, then wrap them around the Almond and Basil Oil Cakes. Place a piece of the wrapped cake onto a plate. Pipe or spoon some Chocolate Lemon Cream, Basil Emulsion, and Raspberry Water Gelée onto the plate in a composition of your choice. Decorate with a few Chocolate Puff Pastry sticks, Raspberry Foam, and basil leaves (if using). Serve immediately.

MINT | Chocolate Cheese Mousse | Hot Orange Carrot Gelée | Fig Mint Confit

Hot Orange Carrot Gelée

½ cup (125 mL) carrot juice
   (see page 186)

½ cup (125 mL) orange juice

1 tsp (5 mL) agar powder

1 Tbsp (15 mL) honey

1½ tsp (7.5 mL) Gelatin Mix
   (see page 185)

Line a 4 x 8 inch (10 x 20 cm) heatproof, shallow container with plastic wrap. Place the carrot and orange juice in a tall and narrow container. Add the agar powder and blend with an immersion blender.

Transfer the mixture into a saucepan, add the honey and bring to a boil. Continue to cook until the mixture begins to thicken, then remove from the heat and stir in the gelatin until dissolved. Immediately strain into the plastic wrap-lined container. Let it set at room temperature. Store the Gelée in the refrigerator for up to 2 days. Serve warm.

Carrot Chips

1 large carrot, peeled

1 cup (250 mL) Simple Syrup
   (see page 187)

Preheat the oven to 200°F (95°C). Using a vegetable peeler or mandoline, slice the carrots into long, thin strands. Bring the Simple Syrup to a boil, then reduce the heat to minimum and poach the carrot strands until they become translucent. Transfer the carrots onto paper towel to remove any excess syrup. Line a baking tray with a silicon mat and lay the carrots flat onto the tray. (For a more interesting presentation, lay the strands over wooden dowels or crunched aluminum foil.) Bake in the preheated oven until the carrots are completely dry (30 to 60 minutes). Store in an airtight container for up to several days.

Chocolate Cheese Mousse

⅓ cup (80 g) cream cheese, room
     temperature

1 Tbsp (15 mL) honey

2 Tbsp (30 mL) whipping cream

4.5 oz (125 g) white chocolate,
     melted

Beat the cream cheese, honey, and
whipping cream with an electric
mixer fitted with a paddle attachment
until light and fluffy. Pour the white
chocolate over the mixture in a steady
stream while continuously beating.
Store in a sealed container in the
refrigerator until set.

Fig Mint Confit

4 Tbsp (60 mL) orange juice

4 Tbsp (60 mL) carrot juice
     (see page 186)

10 mint leaves

7 dried figs, chopped

0.7 oz (20 g) milk chocolate,
     finely chopped

Bring the orange and carrot juice to a
boil. Remove from the heat, add the
mint, and cover with a tight-fitting
lid. Allow it to infuse for 1 hour. Place
the figs and milk chocolate in a food
processor. Reheat the juice infusion,
strain over the figs and chocolate,
discard the mint, and blend the mixture
into a smooth paste. Store in a sealed
container in the refrigerator for up
to 1 week.

Honey Pine Nut Buds

½ cup (80 g) pine nuts

2 Tbsp (30 mL) honey

Preheat the oven to 350°F (180°C).
Line a baking tray with a silicon mat
or paper and toast the pine nuts until
golden brown (about 10 minutes).
Keep warm.

Place the honey in a saucepan and cook
over medium heat until it reaches a
light caramel. Add the warm pine nuts
and mix until all the nuts are coated.
Immediately transfer the mixture back
onto the silicon-lined baking tray. Form
¾ of the mixture into small clusters
in the shape of flower buds using an
oiled fork or knife. Chop or grind
the remaining ¼ of the mixture into a
coarse powder. Store the clusters and
powder in airtight containers.

Assembly

Herb Emulsion (use mint,
     see page 188)

16 fresh mint leaves

Cut the Hot Orange Carrot Gelée into
desired shapes. Top the Gelée with
some Chocolate Cheese Mousse piped
or shaped in the middle and decorate
with a Carrot Chip and mint leaves.
Finish with beads of Fig Mint Confit,
topped with some chopped Honey
Pine Nuts, Mint Emulsion, and Honey
Pine Nut Buds in a composition of your
choice. Serve immediately.

e assembly   Omit the Carrot Chips, Fig Mint
Confit, and Mint Emulsion.
Proceed as above.

ROSE | Chocolate Mango Custard | Rose Lychee Meringue | Coconut Crumble

SERVES 8

Rose Lychee Meringue

½ cup + 3 Tbsp (140 g) granulated
sugar, divided

3 Tbsp (45 mL) canned lychee syrup

2 large egg whites

2 tsp (10 mL) Gelatin Mix
(see page 185)

½ tsp (2.5 mL) rose water extract or
to taste

Bring ½ cup + 1 Tbsp (110 g) of the
sugar and the lychee syrup to a boil.
Continue to cook until it begins to
thicken (around 230°F/110°C).

Meanwhile, whip the egg whites
on medium speed with an electric
mixer fitted with a whip attachment.
When the hot sugar and lychee syrup
begins to thicken, bring the speed to
maximum and add the remaining 2
Tbsp (30 g) of sugar to the whipped
egg whites. Continue whipping for
30 seconds. With the machine still
running, add the hot sugar and lychee
syrup, Gelatin Mix, and rose water
extract. Reduce the speed to low and
continue mixing for 4 to 5 minutes or
until the mixture thickens. Serve warm.

Chocolate Mango Custard

½ cup (125 mL) Fruit Purée
(use mango, see page 186)

½ cup (125 mL) milk

¼ cup (60 g) granulated sugar, divided

3 Tbsp (25 g) custard powder

1 large egg

3.6 oz (100 g) white chocolate, chopped

Bring the mango purée, milk, and 2 Tbsp (30 g) of the sugar to a boil in a saucepan. Whisk together the remaining 2 Tbsp (30 g) of sugar, custard powder, and egg until well combined.

Slowly add the hot milk mixture over the egg mixture, continuously whisking. Transfer into a saucepan and cook over high heat, still continuously whisking, until it begins to boil. Reduce the heat to medium, continue whisking, and cook for 1 minute. Remove from the heat and add the white chocolate. Mix until the chocolate is melted and well combined.

Pour into a clean container. Press a piece of plastic wrap directly on top of the custard and pierce a few holes in the plastic wrap to let the steam out. Let it cool and store in the refrigerator until needed.

Coconut Crumble

4 tsp (20 g) salted butter

⅓ cup (60 g) light brown sugar

1 large egg

½ tsp (2.5 mL) vanilla extract

⅔ cup (100 g) all-purpose flour

pinch baking powder

⅔ cup (60 g) shredded coconut,
unsweetened

Cream the butter and sugar with a rubber spatula until well combined. Add the egg and vanilla and continue to mix until well combined.

Sift the flour and baking powder over the butter mixture, add the coconut and mix until just combined (don't overmix).

Wrap the dough in plastic wrap and freeze until solid (overnight is best).

Preheat the oven to 350°F (180°C). Line a baking tray with a silicon mat or paper. Using the coarse side of a box grater, grate the frozen coconut dough and spread evenly on the baking tray. Bake in the preheated oven until golden brown (10 to 15 minutes). Let it cool and crumble into ¼ inch (6 mm) pieces. Store in an airtight container.

Assembly

16 lychee, quartered

24 to 32 Fruit Chips
(use strawberries, see page 188)

1 cup (250 g) of Strawberry Sorbet
(see page 189)

edible flowers (optional)

Pipe or spoon the Rose Lychee Meringue and Chocolate Mango Custard onto a dish in a composition of your choice. Finish with some Coconut Crumble and lychee quarters. Decorate with strawberry chips and edible flowers (if using). Serve immediately with a scoop of Strawberry Sorbet.

🅔 assembly   Omit the strawberry chips, edible flowers, and Strawberry Sorbet. Proceed as above.

TARRAGON | Chocolate Vanilla Pudding | Caramelized Puffed Rice | Tarragon Emulsion

SERVES 8

Chocolate Vanilla Pudding

1½ cups (375 mL) whipping cream

1 Tbsp (15 g) granulated sugar

4 large egg yolks

1 vanilla bean, seeds scraped

1 Tbsp (15 mL) Gelatin Mix
(see page 185)

3.6 oz (100 g) white chocolate,
melted

Bring the whipping cream to a boil
in a saucepan. In a separate, heatproof
bowl, whisk together the sugar, vanilla
seeds and egg yolks.

Slowly pour the hot cream over the
yolk mixture while continuously
whisking. Cook the mixture over a
double boiler, still whisking, until it
thickens and reaches 185°F (85°C).
Remove from the heat, add the
Gelatin Mix and white chocolate,
and whisk until well combined.

Transfer the mixture in a 9 inch
(22.5 cm) square container lined
with plastic wrap. Let it cool and
store in the refrigerator, uncovered,
to set.

Dried Apricots

8 large dried apricots

1 cup (45 g) fresh tarragon

2 cups (500 mL) water

1 Tbsp (15 g) unsalted butter

Place the apricots and tarragon in a
container fitted with a lid. Bring the water
to a boil, pour over the apricots, and
immediately cover with the lid. Let it sit
for 2 hours.

Remove and discard the tarragon.
Strain and reserve the liquid for the
Dried Cranberries.

When ready to serve, melt the butter in a
frying pan and cook the apricots on both
sides until golden brown. Remove from
the pan and cut into quarters. Keep warm.

Dried Cranberries

1¼ cups (310 mL) reserved apricot tarragon water

½ cup (80 g) dried cranberries

Reheat the apricot tarragon water and pour over the cranberries. Cover and let it infuse for 2 hours. Drain the liquid and reserve for the Gelées.

Firm Fruit Infused Gelée

½ cup (125 mL) reserved apricot, cranberry, and tarragon water

½ tsp (2.5 mL) agar powder

1¼ tsp (6.25 mL) Gelatin Mix (see page 185)

Place the reserved water in a tall and narrow container. Add the agar powder and blend with an immersion blender.

Transfer the mixture into a saucepan, bring to a boil, and continue to cook until it begins to thicken. Immediately strain into a 4 inch (10 cm) square container. Let it set at room temperature. Keep the gelée warm or store in the refrigerator and reheat when ready to serve.

Soft Cranberry Gelée

½ cup (125 mL) reserved apricot, cranberry, and tarragon water

1 tsp (5 mL) powdered pectin

1 tsp (5 g) granulated sugar

Place the reserved water in a tall and narrow container. Add the pectin and sugar then blend with an immersion blender.

Transfer the mixture into a saucepan, bring to a boil, and continue to cook until it begins to thicken. Strain into a container fitted with a lid. Add the rehydrated cranberries and refrigerate until ready to serve.

Caramelized Puffed Rice

1 cup (30 g) puffed rice cereal

2 tsp (10 g) unsalted butter, melted

¼ cup + 1 Tbsp (30 g) Caramel Dust (see page 185)

Preheat the oven to 350°F (180°C). Gently toss the cereal with the butter. Add the Caramel Dust and continue to gently mix until all the cereal is coated. Line a tray with a silicon mat and bake in the preheated oven for 4 minutes. Let it cool and store in an airtight container.

Tarragon Branches

½ cup (100 g) Isomalt (or replace with sugar but cook only to 275°F/140°C)

2 Tbsp (30 mL) water

16 fresh tarragon sprigs

Cook the Isomalt and water in a saucepan over high heat until it reaches 320°F (160°C). Remove from the heat and let it slightly cool. Dip the tarragon sprigs into the cooled Isomalt and shake off any excess, creating strands as it cools. Let them cool completely on a silicon mat, then store in an airtight container.

Assembly

Herb Emulsion (use fresh tarragon, see page 188)

Pipe or spoon a bead of Tarragon Emulsion onto a plate and streak through with a decorating comb. Cut the Chocolate Vanilla Pudding into desired shapes and place 1 piece onto the plate.

Spoon some Soft Cranberry Gelée, onto the plate and arrange the Caramelized Puffed Rice, Dried Apricots, and Firm Fruit Infused Gelée in a composition of your choice. Decorate with an Isomalt Tarragon Branch. Serve immediately.

🅔 **assembly**   Omit the Tarragon Branches, Herb Emulsion and Firm Fruit Infused Gelée. Proceed as above.

Pressure cooking is the operation of cooking in a sealed vessel that does not allow air or liquids to escape below a certain pressure. The early pressure cooker was called a steam digester and was invented in 1679 by a French physicist named Denis Papin. Today, they are referred to as pressure canners, retorts, or autoclaves depending on the industry. Pressure created within the sealed vessel allows water to rise to a temperature higher than its normal boiling point (212°F/100°C). As water's boiling point increases, so does the pressure within the cooker's chamber. Most pressure cookers have an internal pressure setting of 15 psi and a water boiling point of 257°F (125°C). Although there were some safety concerns with early pressure cookers, these were mostly due to improper maintenance. Today's modern pressure cookers are extremely safe and typically equipped with several independent safety mechanisms.

The main advantage of pressure cooking is speed, as cooking at a higher temperature causes food to cook much faster. This is of particular benefit for long cooking processes such as braising or simmering. These methods combine dry and moist heat cooking and require a lengthy period to break down tough connective tissues in cheaper cuts of meats. Typically, without the use of a pressure cooker, a Maillard reaction (browning of meats) is first initiated, followed by a lengthy braising in a liquid, which produces a flavorful sauce. This process can take up to 4 hours. Similar results can be reproduced using a pressure cooker, with a much shorter cooking time—around 40 minutes.

Prolonged cooking in an open-type vessel also increases the loss of volatile aromatic compounds contained within the foods being cooked; the longer the cooking time, the greater the aromatic loss. However, an enclosed chamber will trap more volatile aromatic compounds than an open vessel. And if allowed to cool before opening the lid, an even greater retention will be achieved.

SB³ | PROCESS | PRESSURE COOKING

sweet
spiced | S2S

PEPPER
Chocolate Banana Cream
Pecan Roast | Green Peppercorn Caramel Sauce

ANISE
Chocolate Chestnut Cream
Anise Taro Fritter | Icewine Gelée

CINNAMON
Chocolate Sweet Potato Mousseline
Frozen Pear Mousse | Cinnamon Chips

CLOVE
Milk Chocolate Caramel Confit
Poached Apples | Pecan Clove Brittle

PEPPER | Chocolate Banana Cream | Pecan Roast | Green Peppercorn Caramel Sauce

SERVES 8

Pecan Roast

2.5 oz (60 g) Brioche (see page 187) (or substitute with other sweet bread)

4 Tbsp (30 g) chopped pecans

2 Tbsp (30 g) granulated sugar

1 Tbsp (15 mL) water

4 Tbsp (45 g) icing sugar

3 Tbsp (30 g) cornstarch

1 large egg

3 Tbsp (45 g) butter, melted

Preheat the oven to 200°F (95°C). Slice the Brioche into ¼ inch (6 mm) cubes. Place the cubes on a baking tray and bake in the preheated oven until slightly dry (about 5 minutes). Remove from the oven.

Turn the oven temperature up to 350°F (180°C). Place the pecans on another baking tray and toast until light brown in color (about 5 minutes).

Heat the granulated sugar and water in a saucepan over high heat until it reaches a light caramel color. Remove from the heat, add the toasted nuts and stir until the nuts are well coated. Pour the mixture onto a silicon mat or paper. Let them cool, then roughly chop into ¼ inch (6 mm) pieces.

Mix the Brioche cubes, caramelized pecans, icing sugar, and cornstarch in a bowl until well coated. Add the egg and melted butter. Mix until well combined. Line a 6 x 8 inch (15 x 20 cm) pan with silicon paper. Spread the

batter evenly inside the pan and bake in the preheated oven until golden brown (about 15 to 20 minutes).

Chocolate Roasted Banana Cream

2 medium bananas, peeled

1 tsp (5 mL) freshly squeezed lemon juice

1 Tbsp (15 g) granulated sugar

⅓ cup (70 g) unsalted butter, room temperature

1.9 oz (50 g) white chocolate, melted

Preheat the oven to 350°F (180°C). Place the bananas in the center of a piece of aluminum foil. Coat the bananas with the lemon juice and sugar, then fold in the edges of aluminum foil so it forms a well sealed pouch.

Bake in the preheated oven until the bananas are soft (about 20 minutes). Let them cool slightly. Blend the butter and bananas (and their roasting juice) in a food processor. Add the white chocolate and blend until well combined. Transfer the mixture into a sealed container and let it set in the refrigerator for up to 3 days.

Green Peppercorn Caramel Sauce

2 tsp (10 mL) green peppercorns (from a can and drained)

2 tsp (10 mL) freshly squeezed lemon juice

3 Tbsp (45 mL) maple syrup

½ cup (125 mL) water, divided

¾ cup (150 g) granulated sugar

Combine the green peppercorns, lemon juice, maple syrup, and ¼ cup (60 mL) of the water in a container.

Heat the sugar and remaining ¼ cup (60 mL) of water in a saucepan over medium-high heat until it reaches a light caramel color (320°F/160°C). Remove from the heat and add the lemon juice mixture to stop it from cooking further.

Place the saucepan back over medium heat and cook the mixture for a few minutes to ensure all the sugar is dissolved. Let it cool, then store in a sealed container in the refrigerator for up to 1 week.

Banana Citrus Foam

1.9 oz (50 g) white chocolate, finely chopped

½ cup (125 mL) whipping cream

4 Tbsp (60 g) mashed banana

1 Tbsp + 2 tsp (25 mL) egg whites (about 1 medium)

zest of ½ lemon

zest of ½ orange

Place the chocolate in a tall and narrow container. In a saucepan over high heat, bring the whipping cream to a boil, then pour it over the chocolate and mix with an immersion blender until well dissolved. Add the banana, egg whites, and both zests. Whisk until well combined.

Let the mixture infuse, covered, for 15 minutes. Strain and discard the solids. Pour the liquid into a siphon cream dispenser, insert the nitrous oxide (N_2O) cartridge, shake vigorously, and store in the refrigerator until ready to serve.

Assembly

8 fresh strawberries, thinly sliced

½ strawberry papaya, cubed

32 small leaves fresh mint

32 pieces Crystallized White Chocolate Sticks (optional, see page 186)

Cut the Pecan Roast into desired shapes. Pipe or spoon some Chocolate Roasted Banana Cream onto a plate. Arrange some strawberry slices, pieces of Pecan Roast, and cubes of strawberry papaya in a composition of your choice. Finish with some Green Peppercorn Caramel Sauce, Banana Citrus Foam and decorate with some mint leaves and Crystallized White Chocolate Sticks (if using). Serve immediately.

ⅇ **assembly**   2 whole oranges, segmented

Omit the Banana Citrus Foam, mint leaves, Crystallized White Chocolate Sticks and replace the strawberry papaya with orange segments. Proceed as above.

ANISE | Chocolate Chestnut Cream | Anise Taro Fritter | Icewine Gelée

SERVES 8

Chocolate Chestnut Cream

¾ cup + 1 Tbsp (200 g) chestnut paste, canned

3 Tbsp + 1 tsp (50 mL) grapeseed oil

3 Tbsp + 1 tsp (50 mL) corn syrup

1 tsp (5 mL) vanilla extract

1.1 oz (30 g) milk chocolate, melted

Blend the chestnut paste, oil, corn syrup, and vanilla extract in a food processor until smooth. With the machine running, add the melted chocolate. Continue mixing until well combined. Store in a sealed container in the refrigerator for up to 1 week.

Wheat Starch Dough

½ cup (125 mL) wheat starch flour

4 Tbsp (60 mL) boiling water

Place the wheat starch in a bowl, add the boiling water and immediately mix with a rubber spatula. Knead by hand until it forms a ball. Wrap the dough with a piece of plastic wrap and set aside until needed.

Anise Taro Fritter

⅓ cup + 1 Tbsp (100 g) taro root

2 Tbsp (40 g) Wheat Starch Dough

½ tsp (2.5 mL) baking powder

½ tsp (2.5 mL) anise powder

½ tsp (2.5 mL) sesame oil

1 tsp (5 g) unsalted butter, soft

pinch salt

1 tsp (5 g) granulated sugar

4 cups (1 L) oil for deep-frying

Steam the taro root until soft and set aside to cool. Preheat the oven to 200°F (95°C). Grate the taro root using a box grater onto a baking tray lined with silicon paper. Spread the taro evenly on the tray and place into the preheated oven to dry (about 10 to 15 minutes).

Transfer the taro to a bowl, add the remaining ingredients, except the oil, and knead by hand until it forms a dough. Shape the dough into 8 balls, place them on a tray, cover with plastic wrap, and let rest for 1 hour.

Heat the oil in a saucepan to 350°F (180°C) and fry the taro until light brown in color. Remove with a slotted spoon and drain the excess oil on a paper towel.

Icewine Gelée

1 Tbsp (15 mL) Gelatin Mix
    (see page 185)

6 Tbsp (90 mL) icewine

Place the Gelatin Mix in a heatproof bowl and briefly melt over a double boiler. Remove from the heat, add the icewine, and mix using a rubber spatula. Transfer the mixture into a container fitted with a lid and place in the refrigerator until it forms a gel (overnight is best).

Assembly

3.6 oz (100 g) Chocolate Puff Pastry
    (see page 189)

2 peaches (fresh or stewed)

Preheat the oven to 350°F (180°C). Roll the Chocolate Puff Pastry dough as thinly as possible. Cut the dough into 2 x 1 inch (5 x 2.5 cm) rectangles and place on a baking tray lined with silicon mat or paper. Bake in the preheated oven for about 15 minutes or until done.

Pipe or spoon some Chocolate Chestnut Cream onto a plate. Thinly slice the peaches using a very sharp knife and place a few slices on a plate along with a piece of the Chocolate Puff Pastry, Taro Root Fritter, and Icewine Gelée in a composition of your choice. Serve immediately.

ℯ assembly   Omit the Chocolate Puff Pastry and proceed as above.

CINNAMON | Chocolate Sweet Potato Mousseline
| Frozen Pear Mousse | Cinnamon Chips

SERVES 8

Hot Orange Salad

4 oranges, peeled and segmented

1 cup (250 mL) orange juice

1 tsp (5 mL) agar powder

1 tsp (5 mL) grated fresh ginger

1 Tbsp (15 mL) maple syrup

1½ tsp (7.5 mL) Gelatin Mix
(see page 185)

Preheat the oven to 200°F (95°C). (For
the best results, use a food dehydrator
set at 135°F/58°C.) Line a baking
tray with a silicon mat and lay the
orange segments overtop. Bake in the
preheated oven until the oranges are
warm and slightly dry on the outside.

Line a 5 inch (12.5 cm) square
heatproof, shallow container with
plastic wrap, pack with the warm
oranges and keep warm. Place the
orange juice in a tall and narrow
container, add the agar powder and
blend with an immersion blender.

Combine the orange juice mixture,
chopped ginger, and maple syrup in
a saucepan over high heat. Bring to a
boil and continue cooking until the
mixture begins to thicken. Remove
from the heat and immediately pour
over the warm oranges. Let it set at
room temperature. Refrigerate the salad
until ready to serve. Serve warm.

Chocolate Sweet Potato Mousseline

14.4 oz (400 g) sweet potato (about 1 large)

2 large eggs

⅔ cup (150 mL) whipping cream

⅓ cup + 1 Tbsp (80 g) granulated sugar

½ tsp (2.5 mL) ground cinnamon

2.7 oz (75 g) milk chocolate, melted

Preheat the oven to 350°F (180°C). Place the sweet potato on a baking tray lined with a silicon mat or paper and bake in the preheated oven until soft (about 45 minutes to 1 hour). Let it cool, peel the skin and mash into a purée using a fork or spatula.

Whisk the eggs, whipping cream, sugar, and cinnamon together. Add the sweet potato purée and continue whisking until well combined. Pour into a 6 x 8 inch (15 x 20 cm) pan lined with silicon paper and bake for 30 minutes.

Transfer the mixture in a food processor, add the milk chocolate, and continue mixing until well combined. Transfer the mixture into a container fitted with a lid and place in the refrigerator for at least 2 hours (overnight is best).

Cinnamon Chips

1 small sweet potato, peeled

3 Tbsp (45 g) granulated sugar

1 tsp (5 mL) ground cinnamon

4 cups (1 L) oil for deep frying

Cut the sweet potato into very thin slices using a sharp knife or mandoline. Combine the sugar and cinnamon. Heat the oil to 350°F (180°C) and deep-fry the potato until golden-brown, drain on a paper towel, and lightly sprinkle with the cinnamon sugar.

Sugar Wings

8 tsp (40 mL) demerara sugar

Preheat the oven to 350°F (180°C). Evenly sprinkle 1 tsp of the demerara sugar onto a baking tray lined with a silicon mat. Place another silicon mat on top and bake in the preheated oven for approximately 3 to 4 minutes.

Peel off the top silicon mat. While the sugar is still warm, stretch it into an interesting shape. Cool completely and store in an airtight containers. Repeat the process until you have 8 wings.

Assembly

8 pieces Milk Chocolate Frozen Pear Mousse (see page 186)

Cut the Hot Orange Salad into desired shape.

Place a piece of the Milk Chocolate Frozen Pear Mousse on a plate. Pipe or spoon some Chocolate Sweet Potato Mousseline onto the plate, and arrange a few slices of Hot Orange Salad and Sweet Potato Chips in a composition of your choice. Finish with a Sugar Wing and serve immediately.

ⓔ **assembly**   Omit the Hot Orange Salad and Sugar Wings. Proceed as above.

CLOVE | Milk Chocolate Caramel Confit | Poached Apples | Pecan Clove Brittle

SERVES 8

Poached Apples

2 golden delicious apples

1 cup (250 mL) Simple Syrup
(see page 187)

1 vanilla bean, seeds scraped

1 Tbsp (15 mL) freshly squeezed
lemon juice OR
½ tsp (2.5 mL) ascorbic acid

Peel the apples and reserve the skin for
the sorbet. Remove 8 tubes from the
flesh of the apples using an apple corer
(keep the leftover flesh for the Sorbet
and Confit recipes). Bring the Simple
Syrup to a boil. Add the vanilla seeds,
lemon juice, and apple tubes. Cover with
a tight-fitting lid. Let it sit for at least
1 hour, then refrigerate until needed.

Apple Sheets

2 Tbsp (30 mL) freshly squeezed
lemon juice OR
1 tsp (5 mL) ascorbic acid

1 cup (250 mL) water

1 apple

Combine the lemon juice with the
water in a large bowl. Cut long sheets
from the apple using a vegetable
sheeter, mandoline, or very sharp knife.
As soon as they're cut, place the apple
sheets in the acidulated water for a few
minutes to prevent browning.

Pecan Clove Brittle

½ cup (70 g) chopped pecans

½ cup (100 g) granulated sugar

1 Tbsp (15 mL) corn syrup

4½ tsp (22.5 mL) water

1 Tbsp + 2 tsp (25 g) unsalted butter

pinch ground cloves

Preheat the oven to 350°F (180°C).
Line a baking tray with a silicon mat or
paper. Place the pecans on the baking
tray and toast in the preheated oven
until golden-brown (about 10 minutes).
Keep warm.

In a large saucepan, cook the sugar, corn syrup, and water over high heat until it caramelizes (320°F/160°C). Add the butter, warm pecans, and ground cloves. Stir with a heatproof rubber spatula or wooden spoon until all the nuts are coated.

Empty the sugar and nut mixture onto the silicon-lined baking tray and spread as thinly as possible. Let the brittle cool, then divide in half. Coarsely chop one half with a knife into ¼ inch (6 mm) pieces. Grind the second half into a fine powder using a food processor. Combine the pieces with the powder and store in an airtight container.

Milk Chocolate Caramel Confit

1½ tsp (7.5 mL) freshly squeezed lemon juice

4 Tbsp (60 mL) freshly squeezed orange juice

¼ tsp (1.25 mL) powdered pectin

¼ cup (50 g) granulated sugar

4½ tsp (22.5 mL) water

50 g (3.6 oz) apple flesh (leftover from Poached Apples), finely chopped

pinch ground cloves

3.6 oz (100 g) milk chocolate, finely chopped

Combine the lemon and orange juices with the pectin powder in a tall and narrow container. Blend with an immersion blender until well combined.

Cook the sugar and water in a saucepan over high heat until it caramelizes. Add the finely chopped apples, cloves, and juice mixture. Continue to cook until the mixture begins to thicken and the apples are soft.

Place the chocolate in the same tall and narrow container and pour the hot mixture overtop. Blend with the immersion blender until well combined. Let it cool and store in a sealed container in the refrigerator.

Parmesan Pecan Tuiles

½ cup (40 g) shredded Parmesan

⅓ cup (40 g) finely ground pecans

Preheat the oven to 350°F (180°C). Line a baking tray with a silicon mat or paper. Combine the ingredients, shape the mixture into ½ x 2 inch (1 x 5 cm) rectangles (for best results use a template). Bake in the preheated oven until brown (about 5 minutes). Let them cool on the tray. Remove and store in an airtight container.

Assembly

1 cup (250 mL) Green Apple Skin Sorbet (see page 189)

Arrange a few Poached Apples, Apple Sheets, some Pecan Clove Brittle, Milk Chocolate Caramel Confit, and Parmesan Pecan Tuiles on a plate in a composition of your choice. Finish with a scoop of Green Apple Skin Sorbet and serve immediately.

e **assembly** Omit the Parmesan Pecan Tuiles and Apple Sheets. Proceed as above (store bought vanilla ice cream may be substituted).

Gelling is the operation of solidifying liquids, in a preparation, to different degrees of firmness. The moisture in food is organized by hydrophilic polymers called hydro-colloids, which are naturally present or added to control gelling and thickening. Gelatin is by far the most-used hydrocolloid for gelling; it's prepared by the thermal denaturation of collagen with a very diluted acid.

Gelatin is primarily used as a gelling agent to form transparent, elastic thermo-reversible gels (melts on heating and reforms on cooling). The lower melting temperature of gelatin gels provides its much sought after "melt in the mouth" effect. It's best to allow a gelatin-based preparation to cool slowly (i.e. room temperature to refrigerator) rather than quickly (i.e. hot to freezer). Rapid cooling yields a gel with a weaker structure. When a gel is slowly cooled, the gelatin molecules lose energy gradually, resulting in a stronger gel. Gelatin is perfect for preparations that are meant to be served cold (35 to 39°F/2 to 4°C) and contain a large amount of liquid, such as sweet or savory gelées or foams.

Salt and acid interfere with the bonding of gelatin molecules, whereas milk and sugar increase the gel strength. Gelling alcohol with gelatin is not an issue if the volume is 40% or less. If higher than 40%, other gelling agents should be considered. Making gels with raw kiwi, figs, papaya, or pineapple is not recommended, unless the juice is heated first. Heating the juice will denature the protein digesting enzymes contained in fruit; it's these enzymes that prevent gelatin from forming a gel.

The typical ratio to make a gelatin gel is between 1% and 3% of total liquids. A 1% ratio will result in a soft, and delicate gel whereas a 3% ratio will yield a stronger gel (typically used for gelling mousse-type desserts).

SB⁴ | TEXTURE | GELATIN

sweet
fruity | S₃F

STRAWBERRY
Chocolate Mascarpone Cream
Strawberry Marshmallow | Pineapple Ice Cube

CHERRY
White Chocolate Mousse
Cherry Biscuit | Lemon Confit

PEAR
Milk Chocolate Pear Mousse
Ginger Orange Coulis | Pear Ribbons

RASPBERRY
White Chocolate Raspberry Cream
Jellied Almond Milk | Vanilla Strings

STRAWBERRY | Chocolate Mascarpone Cream
| Strawberry Marshmallow | Pineapple Ice Cube   SERVES 8

Strawberry Marshmallow

6 Tbsp (90 g) granulated sugar, divided

2 Tbsp (30 mL) Fruit Purée (use strawberries, see page 186)

2 large egg whites

1 Tbsp (15 mL) Gelatin Mix (see page 185)

Bring 5 Tbsp (75 g) of the sugar and the strawberry purée to a boil. Continue cooking until it begins to thicken or to 230°F (110°C).

Meanwhile, whip the egg whites on medium speed with an electric mixer. As the sugar and purée are thickening, turn the mixer's speed up to maximum and add the remaining 1 Tbsp (15 g) of sugar. Continue whipping for 30 seconds, then pour the thickened sugar syrup over the egg whites while the machine is still running. Add the Gelatin Mix and when fully incorporated, reduce the speed to low for about 4 to 5 minutes or until the mixture thickens. Serve warm.

Chocolate Mascarpone Cream

¼ cup (60 g) mascarpone cheese

2 Tbsp (30 mL) milk

zest of ½ lemon

2 tsp (10 mL) freshly squeezed lemon juice

4.5 oz (125 g) white chocolate, melted

Place the mascarpone cheese and milk in a heatproof bowl and heat it to 98°F (37°C) over a double boiler or in the microwave. Add the lemon juice, zest and melted chocolate. Whisk together until well combined.

Orange Emulsion

1 Tbsp (15 mL) grapeseed oil

zest of 1 orange

1 oz (25 g) white chocolate, finely chopped

1 Tbsp (15 g) butter

5 Tbsp (75 mL) orange juice

¼ cup (50 g) granulated sugar

1 Tbsp (15 mL) Gelatin Mix (see page 185)

Warm the grapeseed oil in a saucepan over medium heat. Remove from heat, add the orange zest and cover with a tight-fitting lid. Let it infuse for 15 minutes.

Place the chocolate and butter in a tall and narrow container. Bring the orange juice and sugar to a boil on the stove. Add the Gelatin Mix, stir to dissolve, and pour over the chocolate and butter.

Strain the infused oil into the chocolate mixture and mix until well combined using an immersion blender. Refrigerate in a small airtight container for up to 4 days. Serve warm.

Almond Glass

3 Tbsp (45 mL) corn syrup

¼ cup (25 g) almonds, coarsely chopped

Preheat the oven to 350°F (180°C). Line a baking tray with a silicon mat. Dip a 3 inch (8 cm) wide brush in the syrup and paint a rectangular outline about 5 inches (12 cm) long. Lightly dust with some almonds and bake for 5 minutes in the preheated oven. Let it cool completely and store in an airtight container.

Pineapple Ice Cube

¼ fresh pineapple

20 fresh mint leaves

Remove the skin and core from the pineapple. Cut the flesh into ¼ inch (6 mm) thick cubes.

Wrap half of the mint in a cheesecloth (or heavy-duty paper towel) and secure the bag with an elastic. Repeat this same process with the remaining mint. Place one mint bag at the bottom of a tall and narrow plastic container fitted with a lid. Top with all of the pineapple cubes and top the pineapple with the second bag of mint. Seal the container with a lid and let it infuse in the refrigerator for at least 2 hours (overnight is best).

Once infused, remove the mint bags, drain the pineapple cubes and pack them into the cavities of a plastic ice cube tray. Freeze the pineapple until it holds together, but is not completely frozen.

Assembly

½ cup (80 g) Caramelized Nuts (use almonds and crumb, see page 185)

4 fresh strawberries, quartered

8 sprigs fresh mint

Spoon or pipe some warm Strawberry Marshmallow, Chocolate Mascarpone Cream, and Orange Emulsion onto a plate in a composition of your choice. Decorate with a few pieces of Almond Glass and some caramelized almonds/crumb. Serve immediately with one Pineapple Ice Cube topped with a sprig of mint.

e assembly   Omit the Orange Emulsion and Almond Glass. Proceed as above.

CHERRY | White Chocolate Mousse | Cherry Biscuit | Lemon Confit

SERVES 8

Cherry Biscuit

⅓ cup + 2 Tbsp (105 g)
    granulated sugar, divided

½ cup (125 mL) Fruit Purée
    (use cherries, see page 186)

4 Tbsp (60 mL) egg whites
    (about 2 large)

4 Tbsp (60 mL) egg yolks
    (about 3 large)

⅓ cup + 1 Tbsp (60 g)
    all-purpose flour, sifted

Preheat the oven to 375°F (190°C). Bring ⅓ cup (75 g) of the sugar and the Cherry Purée to a boil. Cook until it begins to thicken or to 230°F (110°C).

Whisk the egg whites using an electric mixer fitted with a whip attachment on medium speed. When the foam no longer gains volume and starts to slide from the sides of the bowl, increase the speed to maximum, add the remaining 2 Tbsp (30 g) of sugar and continue whipping into stiff peaks.

Pour the hot cherry mixture over the whites with the machine still running, reduce the speed to minimum, and beat for 1 minute.

Add the egg yolks and gently fold using a rubber spatula. Add the flour and continue folding until well combined. Move the mixture onto a 6 x 8 inch (15 x 20 cm) square baking tray lined with silicon paper. Bake in the preheated oven for approximately 15 minutes. Remove the Cherry Biscuit from the tray and let it cool on a wire rack.

White Chocolate Mousse

2 Tbsp + 2 tsp (40 mL) whipping cream, unwhipped

1 large egg yolk

3½ tsp (15 g) icing sugar

1 Tbsp (15 mL) Gelatin Mix (see page 185)

3.6 oz (100 g) white chocolate, melted

¾ cup + 1 tsp (180 mL) whipping cream, whipped into soft peaks

Whisk the unwhipped whipping cream with the egg yolks and icing sugar in a stainless steel bowl over a double boiler. Whisk continuously until the mixture reaches 185°F (85°C). Remove from the heat, add the Gelatin Mix, and whisk until well combined. Allow it to cool to 98°F (37°C).

Whisk in the melted white chocolate and ¼ of the whipped whipping cream. Add the remaining whipped cream and gently fold with a rubber spatula. Cover and store in the refrigerator until set.

Assembly

1 sheet filo dough

3 Tbsp (45 g) butter, melted

¼ cup (40 g) Caramel Dust (see page 185)

½ cup (125 mL) Fruit Coulis (use apricots, see page 188)

16 to 24 cherries (stewed or fresh)

16 to 24 pieces Lemon Confit (see page 188)

Preheat the oven to 350°F (180°C). Cut the Cherry Biscuit into 1 inch (2.5 cm) cubes.

Line a baking tray with a silicon mat. Brush the filo dough with melted butter, sprinkle the entire sheet with the Caramel Dust and bake until golden-brown, approximately 5 minutes. Briefly cool, then break into small shards.

Pipe or spoon some White Chocolate Mousse onto a plate and arrange the cherries, Cherry Biscuit, Lemon Confit, Apricot Coulis and filo shards in a composition of your choice. Serve immediately.

e **assembly**   3 Tbsp (20 g) Caramelized Nuts (use almonds, see page 185)

Omit the filo shards and Lemon Confit. Cut the Cherry Biscuit into desired shapes and top with some cherries. Scoop or pipe some White Chocolate Mousse over the cake, garnish with some apricot coulis, and a sprinkle of chopped caramelized almonds. Serve immediately.

PEAR | Milk Chocolate Pear Mousse | Ginger Orange Coulis | Pear Ribbons

SERVES 8

Slow Poached Pears

½ cup (100 g) granulated sugar

2½ cups (625 mL) water

½ tsp (2.5 mL) Ascorbic Acid
  (see page 188)

zest of ½ lemon

zest of ½ orange

1 slice fresh ginger

2 pears, peeled, cored, and halved

Bring the sugar and water to a boil. Remove from the heat, cover, and let cool for 10 to 15 minutes. Add the remaining ingredients. Cover and cook over medium heat until the pears are cooked, but still hold their shape (about 1 hour). Alternately, cook in a sealed bag in a 150°F (65°C) agitated water bath (see page 36) for approximately 2 hours (if using this method only use enough syrup to cover the pears). Refrigerate for up to 3 days.

Walnut Ginger Crumble

⅓ cup + 2 Tbsp (90 g) granulated
  sugar

1 Tbsp + 1 tsp (20 mL) molasses

2 Tbsp + 1 tsp (35 mL) honey

3 Tbsp (45 g) unsalted butter

pinch ground ginger

pinch ground cinnamon

¼ tsp (1.25 mL) baking soda

pinch salt

3 Tbsp (45 mL) water

1⅓ cup (200 g) all-purpose flour

1¼ cup (100 g) coarsely chopped
  walnuts

Cream the sugar, molasses, honey, butter, ginger, cinnamon, baking soda, and salt using an electric mixer fitted with a paddle attachment.

Add the water, flour, and walnuts. Mix on low speed until well combined (don't overmix).

Wrap the dough in plastic wrap and freeze for at least 2 hours (overnight is best).

Preheat the oven to 325°F (160°C). Line a baking tray with a silicon mat or paper. Using a box grater, grate the dough on the largest size blade and spread the strands evenly onto the baking tray. Bake until the dough is golden-brown (about 6 to 10 minutes). Let it cool, then crush the cookie strands lightly into small pieces. Store in an airtight container. Note that this recipe makes more than needed, but the unbaked dough can be stored for several weeks in the freezer.

Pear Ribbons

1 Tbsp + 2 tsp (25 mL) freshly squeezed lemon juice

3 Tbsp (45 mL) water

3 Tbsp (45 mL) corn syrup

3 Tbsp (45 mL) honey

1 tsp (5 mL) powdered pectin

5 oz (150 g) drained, canned or poached pears

Combine all the ingredients in a saucepan, except for the pears. Bring to a boil.

Place the pears in a food processor, add the hot liquid, and purée. Transfer the mixture back into the saucepan and cook until it has reduced by ⅓ and reaches a thick, syrupy consistency. Remove from the heat and place the mixture in a metal bowl over an ice bath until cold. Cover and store in the refrigerator.

Preheat the oven to 200°F (95°C). Place a silicon mat over a baking tray. Spread the cold pear mixture onto the tray in 2 inch (5 cm) wide strips (use a template for best results). Bake in the preheated oven until the strips are completely dry (about 45 to 55 minutes). Remove and shape the strips into wavy ribbons. Let them cool, then store in an airtight container.

Assembly

8 pieces Milk Chocolate Frozen Pear Mousse (see page 186)

6 Tbsp (90 mL) Fruit Coulis (use orange juice and ginger, see page 188)

16 mint leaves and/or edible flowers

32 pieces of chocolate shavings (optional)

Place 1 piece of Milk Chocolate Frozen Pear Mousse on a plate. Cut the Slow Poached Pears into ½ inch (6 mm) thick slices and arrange a few pieces along with some orange ginger coulis and Walnut Ginger Crumble in a composition of your choice. Finish with a Pear Ribbon and a few mint leaves and/or edible flowers. Serve immediately.

e **assembly**   Omit the Pear Ribbons and chocolate shavings. Proceed as above.

RASPBERRY | White Chocolate Raspberry Cream
| Jellied Almond Milk | Vanilla Strings   SERVES 8

White Chocolate Raspberry Cream

1 cup (250 mL) Fruit Purée
　　(use raspberries, see page 186)

zest of ½ lemon

3 large egg yolks

2 large eggs

⅓ cup (75 g) granulated sugar

4 tsp (20 mL) Gelatin Mix
　　(see page 185)

3 oz (75 g) white chocolate,
　　finely chopped

Combine the raspberry purée, lemon zest, egg yolks, eggs, and sugar in a saucepan. Continuously whisk over medium-low heat until it thickens (don't let it boil, or it will curdle).

Place the Gelatin Mix and chocolate into a tall and narrow container. Strain the hot raspberry mixture overtop and blend using an immersion blender. Refrigerate until the mixture is set.

Jellied Almond Milk

½ cup (125 mL) White Chocolate
　　Milk (see page 185)

1 oz (25 g) natural whole almonds

1½ tsp (7.5 mL) Gelatin Mix
　　(see page 185)

Combine the White Chocolate Milk and almonds in a high-speed blender. Mix until the almonds are finely chopped. Pour the mixture into a saucepan and bring to a quick boil. Remove from the heat and add the Gelatin Mix. Stir well to combine. Pour the mixture into a container with a tight-fitting lid. Allow it to cool at room temperature for about 30 minutes, then transfer to the refrigerator to set.

Vanilla Strings

3 Tbsp + 1 tsp (50 g) unsalted butter,
　　softened

⅓ cup + 1 Tbsp (50 g) icing sugar

1 vanilla bean, seeds scraped

2 Tbsp + 1 tsp (35 mL) egg whites
　　(about 2 medium)

⅓ cup (50 g) all-purpose flour

Mix the butter, sugar, vanilla seeds, and egg whites using a rubber spatula. Sift the flour over the mixture. Whisk until well combined: Refrigerate the batter for at least 1 hour before using.

Preheat the oven to 325°F (160°C). Line a tray with a silicon mat or paper. Using a piping bag, pipe the batter into 10 inch (25 cm) long strings (don't overlap). Bake in the preheated oven until golden-brown (about 3 to 5 minutes).

Remove from the oven. While the strings are still hot, form each one into a funky shape. Let them cool. Store in an airtight container. *Note: Don't pipe too many strings at one time as you will not have enough time to shape them before they cool.*

Assembly

32 fresh raspberries

32 pieces Caramelized Nuts
　　(use pistachios, see page 185)

8 edible flowers (optional)

Spread some White Chocolate Raspberry Cream in the center of a plate. Pipe a few dollops of Jellied Almond Milk mixture onto the plate. Arrange 4 fresh raspberries, 4 caramelized pistachios, and 1 edible flower in a composition of your choice. Decorate with a few Vanilla Strings. Serve immediately.

e **assembly**　Proceed as above, but pipe the Vanilla Strings into straight lines and bend into simple shapes.

Experimenting with food is key to building culinary memory
— **at least you will know what you don't like.**

2005 MASTERS OF FOOD & WINE: APRICOT, ALMOND MILK & ROSEMARY

bites
crunch | B$_1$C

MERINGUE
Chocolate Lavender Cream
Almond Meringue | Chocolate Apricot Emulsion

DACQUOISE
Lemon Milk Chocolate Cream
Hazelnut Dacquoise Panini | Lemon Confit

NOUGATINE
Chocolate Nut Cream
Chocolate Sucrée | Cocoa Nibs Nougatine

KRISPY
Saffron Milk Chocolate Mousseline
Caramelized Puffed Rice Tuile

MERINGUE | Chocolate Lavender Cream
| Almond Meringue | Chocolate Apricot Emulsion   36 BITES

Almond Meringue

½ cup (125 mL) egg whites
(about 4 large)

½ cup + 2 Tbsp (125 g) granulated
sugar

3 Tbsp + 2 tsp (25 g) unsweetened
cocoa powder

⅓ cup + 1 Tbsp (50 g) icing sugar

½ cup (50 g) ground almonds

¼ cup (25 g) Caramel Dust
(see page 185)

Preheat the oven to 275°F (140°C).
Whisk the egg whites on medium
speed using an electric mixer fitted

with a whip attachment. When the
foam no longer gains volume and starts
to slide from the sides of the bowl,
increase the speed to maximum.
Add the granulated sugar and continue
whipping until it forms stiff peaks.
Add the cocoa powder, icing sugar,
almond powder, and Caramel Dust.
Gently fold in using a rubber spatula.

Fill a piping bag with the meringue
and pipe 1¾ inch (4.5 cm) rounds
onto a silicon mat or paper. Bake for
40 minutes in the preheated oven.
Remove from the oven and cool on
the tray. Store in an airtight container.

Chocolate Lavender Cream

⅔ cup (150 mL) milk

⅔ cup (150 mL) whipping cream

¼ tsp (1.25 mL) dried lavender

2 Tbsp + 2 tsp (40 g) egg yolks
(about 2 large)

2 Tbsp (30 g) granulated sugar

1½ tsp (7 mL) Gelatin Mix
(see page 185)

3.6 oz (100 g) 70% dark chocolate,
finely chopped

Bring the milk, whipping cream, and dried lavender to a boil in a saucepan. Remove from the heat, cover with a tight-fitting lid, and allow to infuse for 30 minutes.

Whisk the yolks and sugar in a bowl. Strain the milk infusion into the yolk/sugar mixture and discard the dried lavender. Whisk until combined.

Cook the yolk/milk mixture over a double boiler, continuously whisking, until it begins to foam and thicken (or reaches 185°F/85°C). Remove from the heat and whisk in the Gelatin Mix. Whisk in the chocolate until well combined.

Transfer into a container fitted with a lid and let it set in the refrigerator for at least 2 hours (overnight is best).

Apricot Ganache

3.6 oz (100 g) 70% dark chocolate,
finely chopped

2 Tbsp (30 g) unsalted butter

4 Tbsp (60 mL) Fruit Purée
(use apricots, see page 186)

4 Tbsp (60 mL) whipping cream

1 Tbsp (15 mL) corn syrup

Place the chocolate and butter into a tall and narrow container. Bring the apricot purée, whipping cream, and corn syrup to a boil in a saucepan, then pour over the chocolate. Blend with an immersion blender until well combined. Let it cool until the ganache has the consistency of soft butter. This recipe makes more than required; the excess can be stored in the refrigerator for up to 2 weeks.

Chocolate Apricot Emulsion

⅔ cup (150 mL) Apricot Ganache

⅔ cup (150 mL) Pastry Cream
(see page 186)

Combine the Apricot Ganache and Pastry Cream in a bowl. Place the bowl over a double boiler and whisk until the mixture is smooth and warm (98°F/37°C).

Dried Apricots

⅔ cup (150 mL) water

½ tsp (2.5 mL) dried lavender

6 dried apricots, cut into ⅛ inch
(3 mm) cubes

Bring the water and lavender to a boil in a saucepan. Remove from the heat and cover with a tight-fitting lid. Allow the mixture to infuse for at least 1 hour.

Strain the mixture and discard the dried lavender. Bring the infusion back to a boil, then remove from the heat. Add the apricots to the pot and cover with a tight-fitting lid. Place the pot in the refrigerator for 4 to 6 hours (overnight is best).

Assembly

9.1 oz (250 g) dark chocolate,
tempered

fresh lavender

Spread a ⅛ inch (3 mm) thick layer of tempered chocolate onto a baking tray lined with silicon paper. Before the chocolate starts to set, cut 3 x 1 inch (7.5 x 2.5 cm) rectangular shapes with a sharp knife. Cover with another sheet of silicon paper or plastic wrap, turn upside down on a cutting board or baking tray, and top with another baking tray (to prevent warping). Let this sit until the chocolate hardens.

Pipe or spoon some Chocolate Lavender Cream into the center of half the meringues. Pipe or spoon some Chocolate Apricot Emulsion into the center of the remaining meringues.

Sandwich a chocolate rectangle between one of the Chocolate Lavender meringue and one of the Chocolate Apricot meringues, leaving at least 1 inch (2.5 cm) of the chocolate extending on one side.

Drain the Dried Apricots on a paper towel and place a small amount on the edge of the chocolate. Decorate with some fresh lavender. If prepared in advance, store in the refrigerator for up 2 hours until ready to serve.

DACQUOISE | Lemon Milk Chocolate Cream
| Hazelnut Dacquoise Panini | Lemon Confit   36 BITES

Hazelnut Dacquoise Panini

2½ cups (200 g) ground hazelnuts, roasted

½ cup + 2 Tbsp (80 g) icing sugar

3 Tbsp (30 g) all-purpose flour

¾ cup + 2 Tbsp (205 mL) egg whites (about 7 large)

½ cup + 2 Tbsp (125 g) granulated sugar

Preheat the oven to 350°F (180°C). Mix the hazelnuts, icing sugar, and flour in a bowl until well combined.

Whisk the egg whites on medium speed using an electric mixer fitted with a whip attachment. When the foam no longer gains volume and starts to slide from the sides of the bowl, increase the speed to maximum, add the granulated sugar, and continue whipping to stiff peaks.

Add the dry ingredients and gently fold in with a rubber spatula. Line a 12 x 16 inch (30 x 40 cm) baking tray with silicon paper. Spread the batter evenly on top of the baking tray. Bake for 15 to 20 minutes.

Lemon Milk Chocolate Cream

¼ cup + 1 tsp (65 mL) milk

3 Tbsp + 1 tsp (50 g) granulated sugar, divided

zest of 2 lemons

3 Tbsp + 1 tsp (50 mL) egg yolks (about 3 small)

1½ tsp (7.5 mL) Gelatin Mix (see page 185)

¾ cup + 1 Tbsp (200 g) unsalted butter, softened

6 Tbsp (90 mL) Milk Chocolate Base (see page 185)

In a saucepan, heat the milk, 1½ Tbsp (25 g) of the sugar, and the lemon zest over high heat until nearly boiling. Cover and allow to infuse for 5 minutes.

Whisk the yolks and the remaining sugar in a bowl until light and fluffy. Reheat the milk and strain over the yolks while continuously whisking.

Pour the mixture back into the saucepan and bring to a boil while continuously whisking to prevent scorching (about 15 seconds). Remove the pan from the heat and whisk in the Gelatin Mix. Cool the mixture to 98°F (37°C) over an ice bath.

Cream the butter in a food processor. With the blade still spinning, add the cooled milk mixture in a steady stream.

Place the Milk Chocolate Base in a tall and narrow container and whip using an electric mixer with a whip attachment to form medium peaks. Add the butter mixture, gently fold with a rubber spatula, and let the mixture set in the refrigerator for at least 2 hours.

Lemon Confit

4 lemons

1 cup + 2 Tbsp (225 g) granulated sugar

½ cup (125 mL) water

Peel the lemons (ensure all the white pith is removed), then section with a sharp knife.

Bring the sugar and water to a boil in a saucepan and add the lemons. Reduce the heat to low and simmer for 15 to 20 minutes. Remove from the heat, cover with plastic wrap, and let it sit for a couple of hours (for the best results, let it sit overnight in the refrigerator).

Assembly

36 sprigs lemon verbena or lemon balm

Cut the Hazelnut Dacquoise Panini into a square shape that fits into your panini grill. (If you don't have a panini grill, use a non-stick frying pan.) Once cooked, remove it from the machine, let it cool, and cut into 2 inch (5 cm) squares. Cut the squares in half and sandwich some Lemon Milk Chocolate Cream in between. Decorate with a wedge of Lemon Confit, and a sprig of lemon herb. Serve immediately.

NOUGATINE | Chocolate Nut Cream | Chocolate Sucrée | Cocoa Nibs Nougatine

36 BITES

Chocolate Nut Cream

3.6 oz (100 g) 70% dark chocolate, finely chopped

1 Tbsp + 2 tsp (25 g) unsalted butter

2 Tbsp (30 g) peanut butter (or you can substitute almond butter, hazelnut butter, etc.)

½ cup (125 mL) whipping cream

1 Tbsp (15 mL) corn syrup

Place the chocolate, butter, and peanut butter into a tall and narrow container.

Bring the whipping cream and corn syrup to a boil in a saucepan. Remove from the heat and pour over the chocolate mixture. Blend with an immersion blender until well combined. Let it cool at room temperature until the filling has the consistency of soft butter.

Chocolate Sucrée

¾ cup (175 g) unsalted butter, softened

⅔ cup + 2 Tbsp (100 g) icing sugar

1 large egg

¾ cup (250 g) all-purpose flour

2 Tbsp + 1 tsp (20 g) unsweetened cocoa powder

Mix the butter and icing sugar in a bowl with a rubber spatula. Add the egg and mix well. Sift the flour and cocoa powder over the mixture and continue mixing with the spatula until well combined.

Wrap the dough in a piece of plastic wrap and store in the refrigerator for at least 2 hours.

Preheat the oven to 350°F (180°C). Line a baking tray with a silicon mat or paper. Roll the Chocolate Sucrée ⅛ inch (2 mm) thick and cut thirty-six 2 inch (5 cm) rounds with a cookie cutter. Place the rounds on the baking tray and bake for 12 to 15 minutes in the preheated oven. Let them cool, then store in an airtight container.

Cocoa Nibs Nougatine

½ cup (125 g) butter

3 Tbsp + 1 tsp (50 mL) milk

2 Tbsp (30 mL) corn syrup

½ tsp (2.5 mL) powdered pectin

1 cup (150 g) icing sugar

1¼ cup (150 g) cocoa nibs

Preheat the oven to 350°F (180°C). Melt the butter, milk, and corn syrup in a saucepan over medium-high heat. Keep warm.

Mix the pectin and icing sugar together. Add to the milk mixture on the stove and cook until it reaches 122°F (106°C). Remove from the heat and add the cocoa nibs. Let cool.

Spoon about 1 tsp (5 mL) of the mix into 1½ inch (3.75 cm) non-stick muffin tins or silicon moulds. Bake in the preheated oven for approximately 5 minutes. Remove from the oven, let them cool, and store in an airtight container.

Assembly

36 fresh raspberries

36 edible flowers (optional)

Spoon or pipe some Chocolate Nut Cream into the center of a Chocolate Sucrée round. Sink a fresh raspberry into the cream. Place this on a plate and lean a Cocoa Nibs Nougatine over the fresh raspberry. Decorate with an edible flower. Serve immediately.

KRISPY | Saffron Milk Chocolate Mousseline | Caramelized Puffed Rice Tuile

36 BITES

Caramelized Puffed Rice

2 cups (60 g) puffed rice cereal

4 tsp (20 g) butter, melted

½ cup (60 g) Caramel Dust
(see page 185)

Gently toss the cereal and butter in a bowl. Add the caramel dust and gently mix until the cereal is coated.

Caramelized Puffed Rice Tuile

3 Tbsp + 1 tsp (50 mL) orange juice

½ cup (100 g) granulated sugar

zest of ½ orange

4 Tbsp + 1 tsp (45 g) all-purpose flour

3 Tbsp + 1 tsp (50 g) butter, melted

1 recipe yield Caramelized
Puffed Rice (above)

Preheat the oven to 325°F (160°C). Whisk the orange juice, sugar, and orange zest in a bowl. Add the flour and melted butter and continue whisking until well combined.

Spoon about 1 tsp (5 mL) of the mix into 1½ inch (3.75 cm) non-stick muffin tins or silicon mould.

Cover the top with the Caramelized Puffed Rice. Bake for approximately 5 minutes in the preheated oven. Remove from the oven and cool. Store in an airtight container.

Saffron Milk Chocolate Mousseline

1 pinch Spanish saffron

2 Tbsp (30 mL) warm water

1 Tbsp (15 mL) Gelatin Mix
(see page 185)

1⅔ cup (400 g) Pastry Cream
(see page 186)

6 Tbsp (90 mL) Milk Chocolate Base
(see page 185)

Soak the saffron in the warm water and infuse for at least 10 minutes. Strain and discard the saffron threads.

Combine the Gelatin Mix, saffron infusion and melt in the microwave or over a double boiler.

If refrigerated, heat the Pastry Cream to 98°F (37°C). Whisk the melted gelatin and saffron infusion.

Whip the Milk Chocolate Base in a tall and narrow container into medium peaks using an electric mixer with a whip attachment. Add the Pastry Cream mixture and gently fold with a rubber spatula. Let it set in the refrigerator for at least 2 hours, overnight is best.

Assembly

chocolate sticks (optional)

gold leaf (optional)

Pipe or spoon ½ of the Caramelized Puffed Rice Tuiles with some Saffron Milk Chocolate Mousseline. Top these with the remaining Caramelized Puffed Rice Tuiles. Move them to a plate and decorate with chocolate sticks and a gold leaf (if using). Serve immediately.

Lecithin is the generic name given to a whole class of fat and water soluble compounds called phospholipids. Lecithin is an emulsifying substance as well as an antioxidant that helps keep fats from going rancid. Lecithin is typically available in a soy-based granular form and enables emulsions or sauces that would otherwise be incompatible. It produces "foamy" presentations that are more stable and incredibly light, such as the "air" made famous by the Adrias in their elBulli restaurant in Spain.

Lecithin is widely used as an emulsifying agent (allowing oil and water to mix and be stable) in many preparations from salad dressings to infant formulas. Lecithin is also the emulsifier used in the production of bulk chocolate to prevent the chocolate liquor and cocoa butter from separating. Lecithin is a very good alternative to egg yolks to stabilize and create fragile, hot emulsions. It provides the same stabilizing properties as yolks, but is not as heat sensitive. The coagulation of proteins in yolks, if over heated, can impart a fairly strong taste along with insoluble particles.

Lecithin is particularly well suited for the aeration process or the operation of incorporating a gas into a culinary preparation. The addition of lecithin to aromatic liquids such as an infusion (i.e. tea), clear broth (i.e. consommé), fruit or vegetable juices (i.e. apple or carrot) along with brisk mechanical agitation (high-speed immersion blender) enables culinary preparations that are light and foamy. Lecithin is cold soluble in most low-fat liquids, but loses its properties in high-fat mediums. Oils or animal fats are rich in triglycerides, which are not good emulsifiers and are likely foam inhibitors. Conversely, amphiphilic (a molecule having a polar, water-soluble group attached to a non-polar, water-insoluble hydrocarbon chain), lipid compounds (i.e. free fatty acids), and proteins (i.e. milk casein or gelatin) are good emulsifiers. Casein and gelatin typically result in foams that are thicker than those created with lecithin.

SB⁵ | TEXTURE | LECITHIN

bites
truffles | B$_2$T

APPLE
Caramel Truffle
Lace & Dust Crisp | Baked Apple

CHERRY
Ancho Truffle
Balsamic Cherries | Crispy Bacon

RED PEPPER
Chocolate Raspberry Ganache
Cocoa Macaroon | Candied Red Pepper

GRAPEFRUIT
Campari Ganache
Crispy Crêpes | Grenadine Grapefruit Confit

APPLE | Caramel Truffle | Lace & Dust Crisp | Baked Apple

36 BITES

Dust Crisp

3 cups (300 g) Caramel Dust
    (see page 185)

Preheat the oven to 350°F (180°C). Line a baking tray with a silicon mat or paper. Using a 1½ inch (3.75 cm) round cookie cutter as a guide, drop ½ tsp (2.5 mL) of the Caramel Dust inside the ring onto the baking tray and spread the mixture evenly using a fork. Remove the ring and repeat this step 107 more times.

Bake in the preheated oven for 3 to 4 minutes. Let them cool before removing from the tray. Store in an airtight container.

Caramel Truffle

8.3 oz (230 g) 70% dark chocolate, finely chopped

2 Tbsp (30 g) unsalted butter, softened

¾ cup (175 mL) whipping cream

2 Tbsp (30 mL) honey

¼ cup (25 g) Caramel Dust
    (see page 185)

Place the chocolate and butter into a tall and narrow container.

Bring the whipping cream and honey to a boil, pour over the chocolate and blend with an immersion blender until well combined. Fold in the Caramel Dust. Let it cool until it has the consistency of soft butter.

Baked Apple

2 small Granny Smith apples, peeled and cored

2 Tbsp (30 mL) orange juice

2 Tbsp (30 g) granulated sugar

Preheat the oven to 300°F (150°C). Cut the apples in half and slice each half into ¼ inch (5 mm) wedges. Place them into a 9 inch (23 cm) square, ovenproof dish. Combine the orange juice and sugar in a bowl and pour over the apples. Cover the dish with aluminum foil and bake in the preheated oven until the apples are soft but still retain their shape (about 30 minutes). Let cool, drain and cut into small cubes.

Lace Crisp

3.6 oz (100 g) wonton or filo dough, sliced into thin threads

1 Tbsp (15 g) vanilla or granulated sugar

2 Tbsp (30 g) unsalted butter, melted

Preheat the oven to 350°F (180°C). Place the wonton or filo dough in a bowl, sprinkle with the vanilla sugar, and toss lightly with the melted butter. Loosely shape strands of the mixture into a circle shapes not exceeding 1½ inches (3.75 cm) in diameter. Set them on a baking tray lined with a silicon mat or paper. Bake in the preheated oven until golden brown (about 3 to 5 minutes).

Assembly

gold leaf (optional)

Place ⅓ of the Dust Crisps onto a platter. Pipe or spoon some of the Caramel Truffle on top of each crisp. Top with another Dust Crisp, more Caramel Truffle, and finish with the remaining Dust Crisps. Let the Caramel Truffle set until firm. Garnish each bite with a few cubes of Baked Apple, gold leaf, if using, and a Lace Crisp.

CHERRY | Ancho Truffle | Balsamic Cherries | Crispy Bacon

36 BITES

Ancho Truffle

1 cup (250 mL) whipping cream

½ dried ancho chili pepper, seeds and stem removed

7.2 oz (200 g) 70% dark chocolate, finely chopped

Bring the whipping cream to a boil. Remove from the heat, add the ancho chili pepper, cover and allow it to infuse until the chili is soft (about 1 hour).

Place the chocolate in a tall and narrow container. Reheat the cream/ancho mixture and pour over the chocolate. Blend with an immersion blender until well combined. Set aside to cool.

Wonton Crisps

nine 3 inch (8 cm) square wonton wrapper sheets

olive oil for brushing

Preheat the oven to 375°F (190°C). Line a baking tray with a silicon mat or paper. Cut the wonton wrappers into 4 equal squares. Brush both sides with oil, then lay them flat on the baking tray.

Bake in the preheated oven until they are golden-brown (about 3 minutes). Cool on a paper towel.

Balsamic Cherries

18 dried cherries, cut in half

2 Tbsp (30 mL) balsamic vinegar (aged 12 years or more)

Place the cherries in a container fitted with a lid. Place the balsamic vinegar in a saucepan over low heat. Once warm, pour the vinegar over the cherries. Cover and soak until the cherries are soft and plump. (This step can be done a few days ahead.)

Assembly

6 slices smoked bacon (maple cured preferable)

small bunch of fresh radish sprouts

1 Tbsp (15 mL) vegetable or olive oil

Preheat the oven to 375°F (190°C). Cut the bacon slices into 1½ inch (3.75 cm) long strips. Place on a baking tray and cook in the preheated oven until crispy. Remove and drain on a paper towel.

Toss or spray the sprouts with the oil.

Place the Wonton Crisps on a platter and pipe some of the Ancho Truffle onto the middle of each one. Top the Ancho Truffle with half a Balsamic Cherry, a piece of bacon, and a few sprigs of radish sprouts.

RED PEPPER | Chocolate Raspberry Ganache | Cocoa Macaroon | Candied Red Pepper
36 BITES

Cocoa Macaroons

6 Tbsp (90 mL) egg whites
  (about 3 large)

4 Tbsp (60 g) granulated sugar

1 cup (100 g) finely ground almonds

1 cup + 2 Tbsp (140 g) icing sugar

1 Tbsp (8 g) unsweetened cocoa
  powder

Preheat the oven to 375°F (190°C). Whip the egg whites using an electric mixer fitted with a whip attachment. As soon as the foam starts to slide from the sides of the bowl and no longer gains volume, slowly add the granulated sugar (continuously beating). Beat until the foam forms stiff peaks.

Sift the ground almonds, icing sugar, and cocoa powder together in a bowl.

Fold the dry mixture into the foam using a rubber spatula and mix well to "deflate" the mixture so that the macaroon will be smooth and shiny once baked. Spoon the mixture into a piping bag fitted with a plain round tube.

Line a baking tray with a silicon mat or paper. Pipe the mixture onto the baking tray in 1 inch (2.5 cm) rounds. Let the macaroons dry out for a few minutes.

Bake for 12 to 15 minutes in the preheated oven. Remove from the oven, let cool on a wire rack and store in an airtight container.

Raspberry Ganache

5.3 oz (150 g) 70% dark chocolate,
  finely chopped

3 Tbsp (45 g) unsalted butter,
  room temperature

5 Tbsp (75 mL) Fruit Purée
  (use raspberries, see page 186)

5 Tbsp (75 mL) whipping cream

1 Tbsp + 1 tsp (20 mL) corn syrup

Place the chocolate and butter in a tall and narrow container.

Combine the raspberry purée, whipping cream, and corn syrup in a saucepan over high heat. Bring to a boil. Remove from the heat and pour over the chocolate. Blend with an immersion blender until well combined. Let it cool until the ganache has the consistency of soft butter.

Candied Red Pepper

1 whole red bell pepper

1 cup (250 mL) Simple Syrup
  (see page 187), heated

Preheat the oven to 200°F (95°C). Char the skin of the red pepper over an open flame (gas oven, blow torch, barbecue). Scrape off the layer of burnt skin, cut the peppers in half, and remove the seeds and membrane. Cut the remaining flesh into thin strips. Place the pepper strips in a shallow container, pour the Simple Syrup overtop and cover with a tight-fitting lid. Let it infuse for 15 minutes.

Remove the peppers from the Simple Syrup and drain on a paper towel. Line a baking tray with a silicon mat and lay the peppers overtop (ensure they don't touch).

Place the baking tray in the preheated oven until the pepper strips are semi-dry (about 20 minutes). Cool and store in an airtight container.

Assembly

Place the Cocoa Macaroons on a platter. Pipe or spoon some Raspberry Ganache on top of each Macaroon and let it set at room temperature until firm to the touch. Decorate each Macaroon with a few strips of Candied Red Pepper.

GRAPEFRUIT | Campari Ganache | Crispy Crêpes | Grenadine Grapefruit Confit

36 BITES

Crispy Crêpes

⅓ cup + 1 Tbsp (60 g) all-purpose flour

4 Tbsp (60 g) granulated sugar

1 tsp (5 mL) powdered pectin

4 Tbsp (60 mL) egg whites (about 2 large)

2 Tbsp (30 g) butter, melted

2 cup (500 mL) water

Preheat the oven to 350°F (180°C). Combine all the ingredients in a large bowl and whisk well.

Spoon ½ tsp (2.5 mL) of the batter into 1¾ inch (4.5 cm) flexible silicon moulds or non-stick mini muffin tins. Repeat until you have made 216 Crispy Crêpes.

Bake in the preheated oven until golden-brown (about 15 minutes).

Campari Ganache

12.2 oz (340 g) white chocolate, finely chopped

3 Tbsp (45 g) unsalted butter, room temperature

5 Tbsp (75 mL) pink grapefruit juice

5 Tbsp (75 mL) whipping cream

1 Tbsp + 1 tsp (20 mL) corn syrup

4 Tbsp (60 mL) Campari liquor

Place the chocolate and butter in a tall and narrow container.

Bring the pink grapefruit juice, whipping cream, and corn syrup to a boil in a saucepan. Remove from the heat and pour over the chocolate. Blend with an immersion blender until well combined. Add the Campari and blend again. Let it cool until the ganache has the consistency of soft butter.

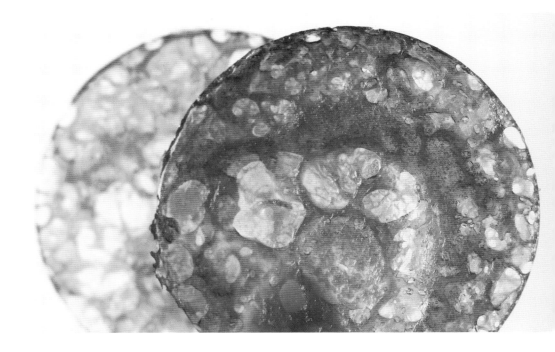

Grenadine Grapefruit Confit

2 pink grapefruits

1 cup (250 mL) grenadine

Peel the skin of the pink grapefruit with a vegetable peeler or sharp knife. Cut the peel into ¼ x 1 inch (0.5 x 2.5 cm) strips.

Bring a pot of water to a boil and blanch the grapefruit peel strips for one minute. Remove the strips from the water and discard the water. Repeat this blanching process 1 more time.

Place the blanched strips in a pot, cover with grenadine syrup, and confit (preserve) over very low heat for 1 hour.

Remove from the heat and let it cool. Store it in refrigerator, still covered in the syrup, until needed. Refrigerated grapefruit confit will keep for several weeks.

Assembly

36 sprigs herbs or edible flowers (optional)

Lay 36 Crispy Crêpes on a tray. Pipe or spoon 1 tsp (5 mL) of the Campari Ganache on top of each Crêpe, top with another Crêpe, then another dollop of Ganache. Repeat three more times and end with a Crêpe.

Let the Ganache set until firm (about 10 minutes). Finish each tower with a few strips of Grenadine Grapefruit Confit and a small sprig of herb or flower (if using).

The general definition of foam is a substance that is formed by trapping many gas bubbles in a liquid or solid. The same process can also be achieved through the incorporation of air via another type of gas—nitrous oxide (N_2O)—using a siphon cream dispenser.

Essentially, foams are the result of mechanically incorporating air into egg whites, which consist almost entirely of proteins and water so that the resulting preparation gains volume and becomes as light as possible in texture. Adding air is not an issue, but past a certain point, excessive beating will break and collapse the foam. Research has shown that in order to gain more volume in a foam from the protein available, more water must be added (typically beaten in after the foam reaches maximum volume). However, the "water" need not be just water but can instead be an aromatic liquid such as fruit juice, wine, or an infusion. This results in many different foams with unique and distinct flavors and colors (i.e. red strawberry foam).

Foams are typically quite fragile and prone to deflation unless stabilized by the addition of a substantial amount of sugar, which makes them unsuitable for savory dishes. However, this issue can be overcome through the use of egg white powder. In this form, the typically freeze-dried egg whites must be reconstituted with water before foaming. By replacing the water with a non-fat aromatic liquid such as vegetable juice or clear stock, you open a realm of possibilities. Note that the less liquid used for rehydration, the more stable the foam will be even without added sugar. Another method is to use a thickened, hot aromatic liquid (i.e. xanthan) and pour it over the foamed, fresh egg whites along with gelatin (as the emulsifier and stabilizer). This results in foam that can be served hot or cold. The amount of gelatin, along with the density and temperature of the liquid, yields foams that are thick like a mousse, fluid like a cream, or liquid like a soup.

SB⁶ | PROCESS | FOAMING

bites

lollies | B₃L

TOMATO
Lemon Almond Cream Cakes
Tomato Confit | Olive Nibs

PASSION
Passion Fruit Ganache
Almond Tuile | Orange Gelée

STRAWBERRY
Strawberry Ganache
Almond Dacquoise | Basil Oranges

PEANUT
Peanut Butter Ganache
Banana Bread | Raspberry Jelly

TOMATO | Lemon Almond Cream Cakes | Tomato Confit | Olive Nibs

36 BITES

Lemon Almond Cream Cakes

½ cup (125 g) unsalted butter,
    room temperature

¾ cup + 3 Tbsp (125 g) icing sugar

zest of ½ lemon

3 large eggs

1¼ cup (125 g) finely ground
    almonds

3 Tbsp + 2 tsp (25 g) flan powder

1 cup + 5 tsp (275 mL) Pastry Cream
    (see page 186)

Preheat the oven to 350°F (180°C).
Cream the butter, icing sugar, and
lemon zest in a food processor. Add the
eggs one at a time. Once incorporated,
add the almonds and flan powder.
Ensure it is well incorporated, then
add the Pastry Cream. Pulse until just
combined (don't overmix).

Spoon about 1 Tbsp (15 mL) of the
batter into 1¾ inch (4.5 cm) flexible
silicon moulds or non-stick mini
muffin tins.

Bake in the preheated oven for 15
minutes. Let the cakes cool on a wire
rack, then store in an airtight container.
This recipe makes more than needed;
leftovers can be stored in the freezer
for several weeks.

Tomato Confit

18 whole cherry or strawberry
    tomatoes, skin removed, halved,
    and seeds removed

3 Tbsp (45 mL) olive oil

1 vanilla bean, seeds scraped

1 Tbsp (15 g) granulated sugar
    or to taste

Preheat the oven to 250°F (120°C).
Place the tomatoes on a baking tray
lined with a silicon mat or paper.

Mix the olive oil and vanilla seeds
together in a bowl and spoon over the
tomatoes. Sprinkle the tomatoes with
the sugar and roast in the preheated
oven until they are semi-dry (about
1½ to 2 hours). Cool and store in an
airtight container. You can make these
several days in advance and keep them
in the refrigerator until ready to use.

Olive Nibs

18 pitted kalamata olives, halved

½ cup (125 mL) Simple Syrup
    (see page 187), heated

Preheat the oven to 185°F (85°C).
Place the olives into a bowl and cover
with the Simple Syrup. Let them soak
for 15 minutes.

Strain the olives and pat them dry with
paper towel. Line a baking tray with
a new paper towel and lay the olives
overtop (ensure they don't touch one
another).

Bake in the preheated oven until dry.
Remove from the oven, cool, coarsely
chop, and store in an airtight container.

Assembly

36 lolly sticks

6.4 oz (180 g) white chocolate,
    tempered

zest of 3 lemons

36 sprigs rosemary

Lay 36 Lemon Almond Cream
Cakes on a tray. Pipe or spoon about
1 tsp (5 mL) of white chocolate on
top of each cake. Lightly sprinkle with
some lemon zest, spike a lolly stick in
the middle, and let the chocolate set
until firm. Garnish with ½ a Tomato
Confit, chopped Olive Nibs, and a
sprig of rosemary.

PASSION | Passion Fruit Ganache | Almond Tuile | Orange Gelée

36 BITES

Passion Fruit Ganache

3.6 oz (100 g) 70% dark chocolate, finely chopped

2 Tbsp (30 g) unsalted butter, room temperature

3 Tbsp (45 mL) Fruit Purée (use passion fruit, see page 186)

3 Tbsp + 1 tsp (50 mL) whipping cream

1 Tbsp (15 mL) corn syrup

Place the chocolate and butter in a tall and narrow container.

Bring the passion fruit purée, whipping cream, and corn syrup to a boil in a saucepan. Remove from the heat and pour over the chocolate. Blend with an immersion blender until well combined.

Let it cool until the ganache has the consistency of soft butter.

Almond Tuile

½ cup (120 g) butter, melted

½ cup (120 g) granulated sugar

1½ cups (160 g) sliced, blanched almonds

3 Tbsp (30 g) all-purpose flour

Preheat the oven to 375°F (190°C). Combine all the ingredients in a bowl and mix with a rubber spatula until well combined.

Drop ⅓ of the dough between 2 sheets of silicon paper, roll to ⅛ inch (3 mm) thickness and cut into 1½ inch (4 cm) rounds with a cookie cutter. Place each circle into 1¾ inch (4.5 cm) flexible silicon moulds or non-stick mini muffin tins and bake in the preheated oven until golden-brown (about 5 minutes). Remove from the oven and let them cool before removing from the mould. Repeat the steps until all the dough is used. Store in an airtight container.

Assembly

1 recipe Fruit Gelée/Jelly (use orange juice, see page 188)

36 lolly sticks

18 cherries, quartered

36 mint sprigs

Pipe or spoon 1 tsp (5 mL) Passion Fruit Ganache into the center of an Almond Tuile and press another Almond Tuile on top. Spike a lolly stick in the center and let it sit until the ganache is set (about 10 minutes). Decorate with some Orange Gelée, 2 cherry quarters, and a sprig of fresh mint.

STRAWBERRY | Strawberry Ganache | Almond Dacquoise | Basil Oranges

36 BITES

Crispy Rings

⅓ cup + 4 tsp (100 g) butter, melted

twelve 8 inch (20 cm) square egg roll wrappers (store bought)

1 cup (200 g) granulated sugar

Preheat the oven to 350°F (180°C). Brush some butter evenly on both sides of the egg roll wrapper. Sprinkle 1 side with sugar.

Cut the egg roll wrapper into 8 x 1 inch (20 x 2.5 cm) rectangular strips. Wrap a piece of parchment paper around a 2 inch (5 cm) wooden dowel, wrap the buttered side against the paper and press the meeting ends to make a good seal.

Bake in the preheated oven until golden-brown (about 5 minutes). Remove from the oven, slide the rings off the dowel and let them cool on a wire rack. Store in an airtight container for up to 2 days.

Almond Dacquoise

1 cup (100 g) ground almonds

¼ cup + 1 Tbsp (40 g) icing sugar

1 Tbsp + 1 tsp (15 g) all-purpose flour

½ cup (120 mL) egg whites (about 4 large)

4 Tbsp (60 g) granulated sugar

Preheat the oven to 350°F (180°C). Mix the ground almonds, icing sugar, and flour together in a large bowl.

Using an electric mixer fitted with a whip attachment, beat the egg whites into stiff peaks. When the foam stops gaining volume, add the sugar.

Add ⅓ of the egg whites into the almond mixture and mix until well combined using a rubber spatula. Add the rest of the egg whites and fold in gently.

Divide the mixture into thirty-six 1¾ inch (4.5 cm) flexible silicon moulds or non-stick muffin tins.

Bake in the preheated oven for about 10 minutes or until light brown. Remove from the oven, cool on a wire rack and store in an airtight container.

Strawberry Ganache

5 oz (150 g) 70% dark chocolate, finely chopped

3 Tbsp (45 g) unsalted butter, softened

5 Tbsp (75 mL) Fruit Purée (use strawberries, see page 186)

5 Tbsp (75 mL) whipping cream

1 Tbsp (15 mL) corn syrup

Place the chocolate and butter in a tall and narrow container.

Bring the strawberry purée, whipping cream, and corn syrup to a boil in a saucepan. Remove from the heat and pour over the chocolate. Blend with an immersion blender until well combined.

Let it cool until the ganache has the consistency of soft butter.

Basil Oranges

3 oranges, peeled and segmented

8 large basil leaves

Alternate layers of orange segments and basil leaves in a container. Cover with a tight-fitting lid and place in the refrigerator for at least 2 hours to infuse (overnight is best).

Assembly

1 recipe Fruit Gelée/Jelly (use strawberry purée, see page 188)

36 lolly sticks

36 small basil sprigs

3 Tbsp (20 g) toasted slivered almonds

Line a baking tray with a silicon mat or paper. Place the Crispy Rings in rows, drop a piece of Almond Dacquoise in the center, and pipe some Strawberry Ganache around the sides and top of the cake to make a seal. Spike a lolly stick in the center and let it sit until the ganache is set (about 10 minutes). Decorate with some strawberry gelée, pieces of orange segment cut on a bias, toasted almonds and basil sprig.

Cocoa Tuile

5 Tbsp (75 g) unsalted butter, softened

1 cup (190 g) granulated sugar

6 Tbsp (90 mL) orange juice

3 Tbsp (30 g) all-purpose flour

1 Tbsp + 2 tsp (15 g) unsweetened cocoa powder

Cream the butter and sugar in a bowl. Add the orange juice and mix. Sift the flour and cocoa powder over the butter mixture and fold until well combined. Cover and refrigerate the mixture for at least 1 hour before using.

Preheat the oven to 350°F (180°C). Wrap a piece of parchment paper around a 2 inch (5 cm) wooden dowel. Place a silicon mat on a baking tray. Spread the mixture inside a 8 x 1 inch (20 x 2.5 cm) rectangular template.

Bake in the preheated oven until golden brown (about 3 to 5 minutes).

Remove from the oven and wrap the tuile strips around the dowel and press the meeting ends to make a good seal. Bake only a few at a time as the tuiles cool quickly and break when being shaped. *Note: templates are easily made from sheets of acetate or thick card stock paper. Use paper versions only once.*

Store in an airtight container until needed.

Banana Bread

⅓ cup + 1 Tbsp (95 g) unsalted butter, melted

¾ cup + 2 Tbsp (170 g) granulated sugar

1 large egg, room temperature

½ tsp (2.5 mL) vanilla extract

2 medium-sized ripe bananas

¾ cup (100 g) finely chopped roasted peanuts

1 cup + 2 Tbsp (170 g) all-purpose flour

½ tsp (2.5 mL) salt

½ tsp (2.5 mL) baking soda

Preheat the oven to 350°F (180°C). Pour the melted butter into a large bowl, add the sugar, and mix with a rubber spatula. Add the egg, vanilla, bananas, peanuts and continue to mix until well combined.

Sift the flour, salt, and baking soda over the egg mixture and fold until just combined. Pour the mixture into a 6 x 8 inch (15 x 20 cm) mould lined with silicon paper.

Bake in the preheated oven for about 30 minutes. As soon as it's done, flip the cake onto a wire rack to cool.

Peanut Butter Ganache

7.2 oz (200 g) milk chocolate, finely chopped

2 Tbsp (30 g) smooth peanut butter

¾ cup (175 mL) whipping cream

2 tsp (10 mL) corn syrup

Place the chocolate and peanut butter into a tall and narrow container.

Bring the whipping cream and corn syrup to a boil in a saucepan. Remove from the heat and pour over the chocolate. Blend with an immersion blender until well combined.

Let it cool until the ganache has the consistency of soft butter.

Peanut Crumble

⅓ cup (60 g) brown sugar

½ cup (80 g) all-purpose flour

½ cup (80 g) Caramelized Nuts, ground (use peanuts, see page 185)

¼ cup + 4 tsp (80 g) softened butter

Combine the brown sugar, flour, and caramelized peanut powder in a bowl. Add the butter and mix with a rubber spatula until well combined.

Wrap the crumble in plastic wrap, shape the dough into a rectangular tube, and place in the freezer.

Preheat the oven to 350°F (180°C). Using the coarse side of a box grater, grate the frozen crumble over a baking tray lined with a silicon mat or paper (make sure the crumble strands are evenly distributed).

Bake in the preheated oven until golden-brown (about 5 minutes). Store in an airtight container.

Assembly

1 recipe Fruit Gelée/Jelly (use raspberry purée, see page 186)

36 lolly sticks

18 green grapes, quartered

36 sprigs fresh mint

Line a baking tray with a silicon mat or paper. Place the Cocoa Tuiles in rows, drop a piece of Banana Bread in the center, pipe some Peanut Ganache around the sides and top of the cake to make a seal. Spike a lolly stick into the center and let sit until the ganache sets (about 10 minutes). Decorate with some Raspberry Jelly, Peanut Crumble, ½ grape, and a sprig of fresh mint.

To innovate one must take risks and know when one fails
— **everything works until it doesn't.**

drinks
hot | D₁H

STRAWBERRY
Dark Strawberry Chocolate
Almond Toast | Hot Strawberry Gelée

CHERRY
White Cherry Chocolate
Chocolate Breton | Cherry Ganache

RASPBERRY
Dark Raspberry Chocolate
Chocolate Marshmallow | Cocoa Crisp

PARSNIP
Parsnip White Chocolate Milk
Coffee Mousseline | Chana Cake

Almond Cream

½ cup (125 g) unsalted butter, room temperature

¾ cup + 3 Tbsp (125 g) icing sugar

3 medium eggs

1¼ cup (125 g) finely ground almonds

3 Tbsp (25 g) flan powder

1 cup + 2 Tbsp (280 g) Pastry Cream (see page 186)

Place the butter and icing sugar into a food processor and mix until well combined. Add the eggs one at a time. When the eggs are well incorporated, add the almonds and flan powder. Continue processing until well blended. Add the Pastry Cream and pulse until just incorporated. This recipe makes more than needed and leftovers will keep for several weeks in the freezer.

Dark Strawberry Hot Chocolate

4 oz (100 g) 70% dark chocolate, finely chopped

1 cup (250 mL) Fruit Purée (use strawberries, see page 186)

1 cup (250 mL) whipping cream

Place the chocolate in a tall and narrow container.

Bring the strawberry purée and whipping cream to a boil in a saucepan. Remove from the heat and pour over the chocolate. Blend with an immersion blender until well combined and frothy. Serve immediately.

Assembly

4 slices of sweet bread, such as Brioche (see page 187) or any milk-based, store-bought bread, such as Challah

⅓ cup (40 g) slivered almonds

1 recipe yield Hot Fruit Gelée sheets, optional (use strawberries, see page 188)

2 strawberries, quartered

edible flowers for garnish (optional)

8 glasses or cups, warmed

Preheat the oven to 350°F (180°C). Cut the Brioche into 1 x 2 inch (2.5 x 5 cm) pieces. Line a baking tray with a silicon mat or paper. Place the Brioche onto the baking tray and spread a generous layer of Almond Cream on top of each one. Sprinkle the Almond Cream with slivered almonds.

Bake in the preheated oven until golden (about 15 minutes). Remove from the tray and set on a wire rack. Cut the strawberry gelée sheet (if using) into desired shapes and place one on top of each hot almond brioche. Decorate with some strawberries and an edible flower (if using). Serve immediately with a glass of hot, frothed Dark Strawberry Chocolate.

Chocolate Breton

¼ cup + 3½ tsp (80 g) butter, room temperature

2 large egg yolks

⅓ cup + 1 Tbsp (80 g) granulated sugar

⅔ cup (100 g) all-purpose flour

1½ tsp (7.5 mL) baking powder

2 Tbsp (15 g) unsweetened cocoa powder

Cream the butter with a rubber spatula. Combine the yolks and sugar in a separate bowl and whisk until light and creamy.

Add the butter to the yolk mixture. Sift in the dry ingredients and fold together using a rubber spatula. Form the dough into a ¼ inch (6 mm) thick square and refrigerate for at least one hour.

Cherry Ganache

3.6 oz (100 g) 70% dark chocolate, finely chopped

2 Tbsp (30 g) unsalted butter, room temperature

3 Tbsp (45 mL) Fruit Juice (use cherries, see page 186)

3 Tbsp (45 mL) whipping cream

1 Tbsp (15 mL) corn syrup

Place the chocolate and butter in a tall and narrow container.

Bring the cherry juice, whipping cream, and corn syrup to a boil in a saucepan. Remove from the heat and pour over the chocolate. Blend with an immersion blender until well combined. Cool the ganache at room temperature until set.

White Cherry Chocolate

3.6 oz (100 g) white chocolate, chopped

½ cup (125 mL) Fruit Juice (use cherries, see page 186)

1½ cup (375 mL) whipping cream

Place the chocolate in a tall and narrow container. Bring the cherry juice and whipping cream to a boil in a saucepan. Remove from the heat and pour over the chocolate. Blend with an immersion blender until well combined and frothy. Serve immediately.

Assembly

4 cherries, quartered

8 fresh mint leaves

8 glasses or cups, warmed

1 recipe yield Hot Fruit Gelée sheet, optional (use cherry purée, see page 188)

Preheat oven to 325°F (160°C). Line a baking tray with a silicon mat or paper. Cut the Chocolate Breton dough into 2 inch (5 cm) squares and place the squares on the baking tray.

Bake in the preheated oven for 8 to 10 minutes. Remove the squares from the tray and set on a wire rack. Pipe or spoon some Cherry Ganache on the cooled Chocolate Breton, top with a half cherry, decorate with a sprig of fresh mint and a piece of cherry gelée (if using). Serve immediately with a glass of hot frothed White Cherry Chocolate.

SERVES 8

Cocoa Crisp

2 Tbsp + 2 tsp (40 g) unsalted butter, room temperature

½ cup (100 g) granulated sugar

3 Tbsp (45 mL) orange juice

1½ Tbsp (15 g) all-purpose flour

1 Tbsp (8 g) unsweetened cocoa powder

Cream the butter and sugar with a spatula. Add the orange juice and mix until well combined. Sift in the flour and cocoa powder. Fold to combine.

Refrigerate the batter in a sealed container for at least 2 hours (overnight is best).

Preheat the oven to 350°F (180°C). Line a baking tray with a silicon mat or paper. Shape the cold batter into 1½ inch (4 cm) squares (for best results use a template).

Bake in the preheated oven for 4 to 6 minutes. Remove from the tray and let them cool on a wire rack. Once cooled, store in an airtight container.

Chocolate Marshmallow

6 Tbsp (90 g) granulated sugar, divided

2 Tbsp (30 mL) water

3 Tbsp (45 mL) egg whites (about 2 medium)

1 Tbsp (15 mL) Gelatin Mix (see page 185)

1 Tbsp (8 g) unsweetened cocoa powder, sifted

Bring 5 Tbsp (75 g) of the sugar to a boil in a saucepan with the water. Simmer until it begins to thicken (around 230°F/110°C).

Meanwhile, whip the egg whites on medium speed with an electric mixer. When the sugar water begins to thicken, turn the mixer's speed to maximum and add the remaining 1 Tbsp (15 g) of sugar. Continue whipping for 30 seconds. Add the hot thickened sugar syrup with the machine still running. Add the Gelatin Mix, and when well incorporated, reduce the speed to low and continue mixing until the mixture thickens (about 4 to 5 minutes). Add the cocoa powder, fold in with a rubber spatula, and serve immediately.

Dark Raspberry Chocolate

3.6 oz (100 g) 70% dark chocolate, chopped

1 cup (250 mL) Fruit Purée (use raspberries, see page 186)

1 cup (250 mL) whipping cream

Place the chocolate in a tall and narrow container. Bring the raspberry purée and whipping cream to a boil in a saucepan. Remove from the heat and pour over the chocolate. Blend with an immersion blender until well combined and frothy. Serve immediately.

Assembly

1 recipe yield Hot Fruit Gelée (use raspberry purée, see page 188)

16 raspberries

8 mint leaves

8 glasses or cups, warmed

Cut the hot raspberry gelée into desired shapes. Pipe or spoon some Chocolate Marshmallow on top of the raspberry gelée. Spike 3 Cocoa Crisps into the gelée and finish with fresh raspberries and a mint leaf. Serve immediately with a glass of hot frothed Dark Raspberry Chocolate.

Chana Cake

¼ cup (25 g) finely ground almonds

¼ cup (25 g) finely ground hazelnuts

⅔ cup + 2 Tbsp (100 g) icing sugar

1 Tbsp + 1 tsp (15 g) chana flour

1 Tbsp + 1 tsp (15 g) unsweetened
   cocoa powder

4 Tbsp (60 mL) egg whites
   (about 2 large)

3 Tbsp + 1 tsp (50 g) Brown Butter
   (see page 188), heated

Preheat the oven to 350°F (180°C).
Combine all the dry ingredients in a
large bowl. Add the egg whites and
mix until well incorporated using a
rubber spatula. Add the Brown Butter
and mix until well combined.

Evenly distribute the batter into sixteen
1¾ inch (4.5 cm) round, flexible
moulds or non-stick muffin tins.

Bake in the preheated oven for 20
minutes. Remove from the oven and
let it cool for a few minutes before
removing from the moulds. This recipe
makes more than needed. Leftovers will
keep for several weeks in the freezer.

Coffee Glass

1 tsp (5 mL) instant coffee

1 tsp (5 mL) hot water

2 Tbsp (30 mL) corn syrup

Preheat the oven to 350°F (180°C).
Line a baking tray with a silicon mat.
Dissolve the coffee in the hot water
and mix in the corn syrup. Using a
1 inch (2.5 cm) wide brush, dip into
the mixture, and paint lines on the
baking tray.

Bake in the preheated oven for 3 to 5
minutes. Remove from the oven and let
it cool for about 30 seconds. Remove
from the tray and shape (if desired).
Store in an airtight container.

Coffee Mousseline

1 cup (250 mL) whipping cream

¼ cup (20 g) whole coffee beans

3 Tbsp (45 g) granulated sugar

Place the whipping cream and coffee
beans in a container fitted with a
lid. Let this infuse overnight in the
refrigerator. Strain the cream, discard
the beans, add the sugar and whip into
soft peaks using an electric mixer.

Parsnip White Chocolate Milk

¼ lb (125 g) parsnips, peeled

7 Tbsp (105 mL) whipping cream

3 Tbsp (45 mL) White Chocolate Milk
   (see page 185)

Steam or pressure-cook the parsnips
until the flesh is very soft. Pass it
through a fine sieve (ensure that you end
up with 4 oz/100 g). Place the mashed
parsnips in a tall and narrow container.

Bring the whipping cream and White
Chocolate Milk to a boil in a saucepan.
Remove from the heat and pour over
the parsnip. Blend with an immersion
blender until well combined and frothy.
Serve immediately.

Assembly

8 glasses or cups, warmed

8 seedless green grapes, peeled

¼ cup (30 g) cocoa nibs
   (see page 202 for resources)

Serve the hot Parsnip White
Chocolate Milk with a Chana Cake,
fresh grape, and Coffee Mousseline
sprinkled with some cocoa nibs on
the side. Decorate with a piece of
Coffee Glass and serve immediately.
Instruct your guests to mix the Coffee
Mousseline into the hot Parsnip
White Chocolate Milk and eat along
with the cake topped with a grape.

Various compounds called "gums" have recently become increasingly popular in modern cuisine. Gums are derived from plants and are generally complex carbohydrates made of different sugar molecules. They are used as thickeners, emulsifiers, and sometimes as gelling agents. In the health food industry, they are used as a fat substitute by providing the "mouth feel" of fat, but without the calories.

Some of the most common gums include arabic gum, guar gum, locust bean gum, and xanthan gum. Typically, sauces and cream type preparations are thickened with cornstarch or flour through a process called gelatinization whereby the starch and liquid are heated to the boiling point and cooked for a certain amount of time in order for the starch granules to swell and thicken the liquid. The disadvantage of this process is that, typically, larger amount of thickener must be added, which affects the final taste of the product. The liquid must also be boiled, which increases the loss of volatile aromas. Conversely, unlike starches, minute amounts of gums are required due to their very high viscosity/thickening properties, which results in a "clean" preparation with its original flavors left unaltered. Minimal or sometimes even no heat is required to achieve the desired thickness, which helps maintain appearance and reduce aroma loss.

Xanthan is a long chain polysaccharide with similar properties to more familiar polysaccharides such as corn starch. Xanthan can drastically increase the viscosity of a liquid with as little as 1% and a typical ratio is 0.5%, but can be as low as 0.05%. The higher the shearing (mixing) speed, the lower the viscosity (or a process referred to a pseudoplasticity), which results in liquids that are thickened and stable, but don't seem thick and heavy in the mouth. Xanthan is very stable and can be added in the presence of acid, salt, and sugar without affecting its thickening ability. Xanthan also prevents syneresis or "weeping" (separation of the liquid from solids), which protects many elements, like the crispness of a crust.

S B 7 | T E X T U R E | X A N T H A N

drinks
frappé | D₂F

PEANUT
Peanut Butter Milk Chocolate
Soft Peanut Meringue | Peanut Tuile

COCONUT
White Chocolate Coconut Milk
Pineapple Gelée | Coconut Profiterole

BANANA
Banana Dark Chocolate
Caramelized Banana | Banana Bread Crouton

ORANGE
Orange Milk Chocolate
Orange Gelée | Galangal Baba

PEANUT | Peanut Butter Milk Chocolate | Soft Peanut Meringue | Peanut Tuile

SERVES 8

Soft Peanut Meringue

4 Tbsp (60 mL) egg whites
(about 2 large)

¼ cup + 1 Tbsp (60 g) granulated
sugar

2 Tbsp + 1½ tsp (20 g) finely
crushed roasted peanuts

Preheat the oven to 250°F (120°C).
Whip the egg whites using an electric
mixer fitted with a whip attachment.
As soon as the foam no longer gains
volume and starts to slide from the sides
of the bowl, slowly add the granulated
sugar. Beat until the foam forms stiff
peaks. Fold in the crushed peanuts.

Evenly distribute the mixture into
twelve 1½ inch (4 cm) round, flexible
moulds or non-stick muffin tins.

Bake in the preheated oven for
12 minutes. Remove from the oven,
let them rest for few minutes to cool,
then remove from the moulds.
Serve immediately.

Peanut Tuile

½ cup (80 g) finely crushed
roasted peanuts

1½ Tbsp (15 g) all-purpose flour

¼ cup (50 g) granulated sugar

1 Tbsp (15 mL) corn syrup

4 tsp (20 mL) milk

1 small egg

Combine the peanuts, flour, and
granulated sugar in a food processor.
Mix until well combined.

Heat the corn syrup and milk in a
saucepan over medium-low heat until
just warm. Remove from the heat and
pour on top of the peanut mixture.
Pulse until well combined (but don't
overmix). Add the egg and pulse briefly

until just combined. Refrigerate the
mixture for at least 1 hour.
*Note: this recipe yields more than needed and
leftovers can be kept in the refrigerator for up
to 1 week or for several weeks in the freezer.*

Preheat the oven to 350°F (180°C).
Place a 2 inch (5 cm) round, hollow
template on top of a silicon mat or
paper. *Note: Templates are easily made from
sheets of acetate or thick card stock paper.
Use paper versions only once.* Spread the
mixture within the template as evenly
as possible to ⅛ inch (3 mm) thickness.
Carefully remove the template and
repeat the process until you have
completed 16 tuiles.

Bake in the preheated oven until
golden-brown (about 3 to 5
minutes). Remove from the oven
and cool on a wire rack. Store in
an airtight container.

Peanut Butter Milk Chocolate

¾ cup (250 g) Milk Chocolate Base
(see page 185)

¼ cup (50 g) smooth peanut butter

1 cup (250 mL) White Chocolate
Milk (see page 185)

¼ lb (125 g) ice cubes

4 Tbsp (60 mL) white rum (optional)

Place all the ingredients into a
high-speed blender and mix until
well combined. Serve immediately.

Assembly

8 chilled glasses

1 Tbsp (8 g) chopped roasted
peanuts

16 white chocolate shavings
(optional)

Sandwich 1 Soft Peanut Meringue
between 2 Peanut Tuiles and sprinkle
some chopped peanuts on top.
Decorate with some white chocolate
shavings (if using), and serve
immediately with a glass of Peanut
Butter Milk Chocolate.

COCONUT | White Chocolate Coconut Milk | Pineapple Gelée | Coconut Profiterole

SERVES 8

Coconut Profiterole

4 Tbsp (60 mL) water

4 Tbsp (60 mL) unsweetened coconut milk

pinch of salt

2 Tbsp (30 g) unsalted butter

⅓ cup + 2 Tbsp (70 g) all-purpose flour

2 large eggs

2 Tbsp (30 mL) shredded coconut (optional)

Preheat the oven to 375°F (190°C). Combine the water, coconut milk, salt, and butter in a saucepan over medium heat. Once the butter is melted, increase the heat to high and bring to a boil. Remove the pan from the heat, add the flour, and immediately stir until well combined. Bring it back over medium heat and continue mixing for about 1 minute to dry the mixture. Remove from the heat and whisk in the eggs, one at a time, until the mixture is smooth and shiny.

Line a baking tray with a silicon mat or paper. Pipe or spoon the mixture into 1½ inch (4 cm) wide mounds. Sprinkle with some shredded coconut (if using).

Bake in the preheated oven for 14 to 16 minutes. Reduce the oven temperature to 350°F (180°C) and bake for another 6 to 8 minutes. Remove from the oven and let them cool on a wire rack. This recipe makes more than required and leftovers can be stored frozen for several weeks.

Pineapple Gelée

5 Tbsp (75 mL) Fruit Juice (use pineapple, see page 186)

1½ tsp (7.5 mL) Gelatin Mix (see page 185)

Bring the fresh pineapple juice to a boil for 30 seconds, add the Gelatin Mix, and stir until completely dissolved. Transfer the mixture into a shallow container. Cover with a tight-fitting lid and refrigerate until set.

White Chocolate Coconut Milk

¾ cup (175 mL) Milk Chocolate Base (see page 185)

4 Tbsp (60 mL) unsweetened coconut milk

1 cup (250 mL) White Chocolate Milk (see page 185)

¼ lb (125 g) ice cubes

4 Tbsp (60 mL) kirsch (optional)

Place all of the ingredients in a high-speed blender and mix until well combined.

Assembly

eight 1½ x 1 inch (4 x 2.5 cm) slices fresh pineapple

⅔ cup (150 g) Pastry Cream (see page 186)

zest of 1 lime (optional)

8 chilled glasses

Cut the Coconut Profiteroles in half. In the bottom half, pipe or spoon some Pastry Cream. Top with a slice of fresh pineapple and some Pineapple Gelée. Decorate with some lime zest (if using), cover with the Profiterole top and serve immediately with a glass of White Chocolate Coconut Milk.

BANANA | Banana Dark Chocolate | Caramelized Banana | Banana Bread Crouton
SERVES 8

Banana Bread Crouton

⅓ cup + 1 Tbsp (95 g) unsalted butter, melted

¾ cup + 2 Tbsp (170 g) granulated sugar

1 large egg, room temperature

½ tsp (2.5 mL) vanilla extract

2 ripe bananas, mashed

¾ cup (100 g) finely chopped walnuts

1 cup + 2 Tbsp (170 g) all-purpose flour

½ tsp (2.5 mL) salt

½ tsp (2.5 mL) baking soda

Preheat the oven to 350°F (180°C). Pour the melted butter into a bowl, add the sugar and mix with a rubber spatula. Add the egg, vanilla, bananas, and walnuts. Mix until well combined. Sift in the flour, salt, and baking soda and fold until just combined (don't overmix). Pour the mixture into a 6 x 8 inch (15 x 20 cm) mould lined with silicon paper.

Bake in the preheated oven for 45 minutes. As soon as you pull it out of the oven, flip the cake onto a wire rack to cool. This recipe makes more than required and leftovers can be stored in the freezer for several weeks.

Caramelized Banana

1 banana

2 Tbsp (30 g) granulated sugar

Place a non-stick pan over medium-high heat. Peel and slice the banana into 1 inch (2.5 cm) rounds. Sprinkle the banana with the sugar. Caramelize the pieces of banana in the preheated pan on one side. (This step should be done just before serving.)

Banana Dark Chocolate

1 cup (250 mL) Dark Chocolate Base (see page 185)

1 cup (250 mL) White Chocolate Milk (see page 185)

1 medium ripe banana

¼ lb (125 g) ice cubes

4 Tbsp (60 mL) dark rum (optional)

Place all of the ingredients in a high-speed blender and mix until well combined.

Assembly

8 to 16 fresh blueberries

2 Tbsp (30 g) butter, melted

edible flowers (optional)

8 chilled glasses

Cut the Banana Bread Crouton into 1¼ x 1 inch (3 x 2.5 cm) rectangles (½ inch/1 cm thick). Lightly brush both sides of the Banana Bread with the butter and toast on both sides in a frying pan. Top each Banana Bread Crouton with a slice of Caramelized Banana, 1 or 2 blueberries, edible flowers (if using) and serve immediately with a glass of Banana Dark Chocolate.

ORANGE | Orange Milk Chocolate | Orange Gelée | Galangal Baba

SERVES 8

Orange Gelée

½ cup (125 mL) orange juice, divided

1 Tbsp (15 mL) Gelatin Mix
    (see page 185)

1½ tsp (7.5 mL) Cointreau (optional)

Heat ¼ cup (60 mL) of the orange juice in the microwave. Add the Gelatin Mix and stir until completely dissolved. Add the remaining orange juice and the Cointreau (if using) and stir again, pour this mixture in a container fitted with a lid and let it set in the refrigerator for about 2 hours or until firm (overnight is best).

Baba

3 Tbsp + 1 tsp (50 mL) milk, warm

1 tsp (5 mL) dry yeast

1¼ cup (200 g) all-purpose flour

4 tsp (20 g) granulated sugar

1 tsp (5 g) salt

2 large eggs

3 Tbsp (45 g) butter, soft

zest of 1 orange

Place the milk in the bowl of an electric mixer. Dissolve the yeast in the milk. Fit the machine with a dough hook attachment and add the flour, sugar, and salt. Mix on low speed until a dough ball forms.

With the mixer running, add the eggs one at a time. Add the butter and orange zest and continue mixing until well incorporated.

Cover the bowl with a clean cloth and set in a warm place away from drafts. Allow the dough to rise until it doubles in size, then punch it down.

Preheat the oven to 400°F (200°C). Place 1¼ inch (3 cm) balls of the dough into silicon moulds or non-stick mini muffin tins.

Bake in the preheated oven until golden-brown (about 20 minutes). Remove from the moulds and cool on a wire rack. This recipe makes more than needed and the remaining Baba can be stored in the freezer for several weeks.

Galangal Soaking Syrup

2 cups (500 mL) water

1 cup (250 g) granulated sugar

1 large galangal root, peeled
    and shaved

⅓ cup (75 mL) fresh juice orange

Place all the ingredients in a saucepan and bring to a boil. Reduce the heat to low. Cover and simmer until the galangal is translucent (about 30 minutes). Strain the mixture and store the syrup and galangal in separate covered containers in the refrigerator.

Orange Milk Chocolate

1 cup (250 mL) Milk Chocolate Base
    (see page 185)

¾ cup + 2 Tbsp (205 mL) White
    Chocolate Milk (see page 185)

½ cup + 2 Tbsp (155 mL) fresh
    orange juice

¼ lb (125 g) ice cubes

4 Tbsp (60 mL) Cointreau (optional)

Place all of the ingredients in a high-speed blender and mix until well combined.

Assembly

1 green apple, cored

1 orange, peeled and segmented

8 chilled glasses

Pat the orange segments dry with a paper towel and cut on a bias into 3 pieces.

Place 8 Baba in the Galangal Soaking Syrup and press them down until all their air escape and they have absorbed the maximum amount syrup. Remove them from the syrup and drain on a wire rack.

Cut the apple into matchsticks, soak them in the cold syrup, remove, and drain the excess syrup. Cut the soaked Baba in half and place a few pieces of orange on the bottom half. Top the orange slices with some Orange Gelée and a few apple matchsticks. Cover with the other half of the Baba. Decorate with a few strands of finely chopped galangal (alternately, soak the chopped galangal in some grenadine syrup for a different color presentation) and serve immediately with a glass of Orange Milk Chocolate.

Cocoa butter is the natural fat of the cacao bean and one of the most stable fats. It contains natural antioxidants that prevent rancidity and has a shelf life of several years at room temperature.

Although cocoa butter is not a gelling agent per se, it can provide similar functions, in fruit mousses for example, while offering different taste and/or texture profiles. One of the major advantages of cocoa butter over gelatin is that the fat molecules of cocoa butter bind together with that of whipped cream forming a very smooth, fast melting matrix that does not form holes. Note that it is gelatin that gives mousses their "spongy" look full of small holes. Gelatin's suction properties create these holes by leaving empty cavities in the matrix in place of water. Cocoa butter still has the ability to trap the water and provides enough structure and firmness to a mousse like gelatin, but unlike gelatin cocoa butter doesn't have a suction ability. Thus, such mousses will not contract or cave in over their allocated shelf life. Strict attention must be paid to temperature when gelling with cocoa butter; the liquid (i.e. fruit purée) and melted cocoa butter must be at 50°F (25°C) before combining so that they fuse together uniformly.

When solid, cocoa butter has only a mild chocolate flavor and aroma, making it suitable for a modern, savory cuisine. Unlike butter or olive oil, the flavor of cocoa dissipates when heated and does not transfer to the food, resulting in a cooked product with a more natural or unaltered flavor. Cocoa butter has a high smoke point of about 400°F (200°C) as opposed to raw butter at around 225°F (105°C) and a lot less is needed to prevent sticking when searing at high heat. Cocoa butter also has an insulating (coating) property particularly beneficial in reducing shrinkage when cooking expensive foods high in water such as fish or shellfish. The natural stabilizing properties of cocoa butter make it a great alternative, or adjunct, to fats when used in emulsions yielding sauces or other similar preparations that require stability for a longer period, especially if they are to be kept warm.

SB⁸ | TEXTURE | COCOA BUTTER

drinks
cocktail | D₃C

KAHLUA
Whipped Milk Chocolate
Coffee Crystals | Chocolate Lady Fingers

CURAÇAO
Whipped Almond Chocolate
Strawberry Crystals | Chocolate Mascarpone Cake

RUM
Whipped White Chocolate
Pineapple Crystals | Pineapple Meringue

GIN
Dark Chocolate Consommé
Semi-Candied Kalamata Olives | Chocolate Olive Madeleine

KAHLUA | Whipped Milk Chocolate | Coffee Crystals | Chocolate Lady Fingers
SERVES 8

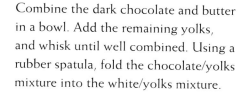

Coffee Crystals

1½ cups (375 mL) water

½ cup (30 g) ground coffee

2 Tbsp + 1 tsp (35 mL) corn syrup

Bring the water to a boil in a saucepan. Remove from the heat and immediately add the coffee. Cover the saucepan, and let it infuse for 15 minutes.

Strain the mixture into a bowl using a coffee filter and discard the ground coffee. Add the corn syrup to the brewed coffee and mix until dissolved. Pour the mixture into a shallow plastic container and freeze until solid (overnight is best).

Whipped Milk Chocolate

3.2 oz (90 g) milk chocolate, finely chopped

1 cup (250 mL) whipping cream

Place the chocolate in a tall and narrow container. Bring the whipping cream to a boil in a saucepan. Remove from the heat and pour over the chocolate. Blend using an immersion blender.

Store in the refrigerator until the mixture is cooled (about 35°F/2°C).

Just before serving, whip the mixture into a soft mousse consistency (medium peaks) using an electric mixer fitted with a whip attachment.

Chocolate Lady Fingers

4 Tbsp (60 mL) egg whites (about 2 large)

2 Tbsp (30 g) granulated sugar

2 Tbsp + 2 tsp (40 mL) egg yolks (about 2 large)

2 oz (50 g) 55 % dark chocolate, melted

1 Tbsp + 1 tsp (20 g) unsalted butter, melted

4½ tsp (15 g) all-purpose flour

2 Tbsp (15 g) cornstarch

3½ tsp (10 g) unsweetened cocoa powder

icing sugar, for dusting

Preheat the oven to 350°F (180°C). Using an electric mixer fitted with a whip attachment, whisk the egg whites to stiff peaks, adding the sugar near the end. Add ⅔ of the yolks into the whites and whip until just combined.

Combine the dark chocolate and butter in a bowl. Add the remaining yolks, and whisk until well combined. Using a rubber spatula, fold the chocolate/yolks mixture into the white/yolks mixture.

Sift the flour, cornstarch, and cocoa powder together, then fold into the chocolate egg mixture.

Transfer this mixture into a piping bag fitted with a 1½ inch (4 cm) round tip and pipe finger-shaped lines on a baking tray lined with silicon paper. Dust with icing sugar.

Bake in the preheated oven for 10 minutes. Remove from the oven and let them cool. Store in an airtight container. This recipe makes more than needed and leftovers can be stored in the freezer for several weeks.

Assembly

8 cocktail glasses, chilled

1 Tbsp (15 mL) Caramel Dust (see page 185)

1 recipe Alcohol Gel, (use Kahlua, see page 185)

8 milk chocolate shavings (optional)

Using a fork, scrape the frozen Coffee Crystals into small shavings and spoon approximately 1 Tbsp (15 mL) into each glass. Spoon some Kahlua gel along side the Coffee Crystals. Spoon or pipe a dollop of Whipped Milk Chocolate on a spoon and sprinkle with some Caramel Dust. Finish with a piece of chocolate shaving (if using). Serve immediately with a few Chocolate Lady Fingers on the side.

CURAÇAO | Whipped Almond Chocolate
| Strawberry Crystals | Chocolate Mascarpone Cake   SERVES 8

Strawberry Crystals

1 lb (500 g) frozen strawberries

2 Tbsp + 2 tsp (40 mL) corn syrup

Place the frozen strawberries in a colander, put a dish with a heavy weight on top (i.e. canned goods), and another container underneath the colander to collect the strawberry water (make sure the colander does not sit directly in the juice). Let it sit at room temperature for 2 hours to partly thaw, then transfer to the refrigerator to thaw completely (overnight).

Heat 4 Tbsp (60 mL) of the strawberry water in the microwave. Add the corn sugar, and mix until well combined. Add the rest of the strawberry water and pour the mixture into a shallow plastic container. Cover and freeze until solid (overnight is best).

Whipped Almond Chocolate

1 cup (250 mL) whipping cream

1/3 cup (40 g) almonds

3.6 oz (100 g) white chocolate, chopped

Bring the whipping cream to a boil in a saucepan. Remove from the heat and add the almonds. Cover and let it infuse for 15 minutes.

Bring the whipping cream back to a boil, then pour into an high-speed blender and blend until the almonds are finely chopped. Add the chocolate and blend until well combined.

Store in the refrigerator until the mixture is cooled (about 35°F/2°C). Just before serving, whip the mixture into a soft mousse consistency (medium peaks) using an electric mixer fitted with a whip attachment.

Chocolate Mascarpone Cake

2/3 cup (100 g) all-purpose flour

1 Tbsp (8 g) unsweetened cocoa powder

1/2 tsp (2.5 mL) baking powder

1/4 tsp (1.25 mL) baking soda

pinch of salt

1/2 tsp (2.5 mL) ground cinnamon

3 Tbsp + 1 tsp (50 g) unsalted butter, room temperature

1/3 cup (75 g) packed brown sugar

4 Tbsp (60 g) granulated sugar

1 large egg, room temperature

1/2 tsp (2.5 mL) vanilla extract

3 Tbsp (45 mL) milk

1/2 cup (125 g) mascarpone cheese

Preheat the oven to 350°F (180°C). Sift the flour, cocoa powder, baking powder, baking soda, salt, and cinnamon into a stainless steel bowl.

In another bowl, cream the butter and both sugars until light and fluffy using an electric mixer fitted with a paddle attachment.

Add the egg to the electric mixer and mix until well combined. Add the vanilla extract and milk.

Using a rubber spatula, fold in the mascarpone cheese, and then the dry ingredients (don't overmix).

Evenly distribute the mixture into sixteen 1¾ inch (4.5 cm) flexible silicon moulds or muffin tins.

Bake in the preheated oven for 10 minutes. Remove from the oven and cool on a wire rack. This recipe makes more than needed and leftovers can be stored in the freezer for several weeks.

Assembly

8 chilled cocktail glasses

1 recipe Alcohol Gel, (use curaçao, see page 185)

4 strawberries, cut into small cubes

1 Tbsp (15 mL) chopped roasted almond

edible flowers for garnish (optional)

Using a fork, scrape the frozen Strawberry Crystals into small shavings and spoon approximately 1 Tbsp (15 mL) into each glass. Spoon some curaçao gel alongside the Strawberry Crystals. Spoon or pipe a dollop of Whipped Almond Chocolate on half of a spoon and fill the other half with strawberry cubes. Sprinkle with some toasted almonds. Decorate with some edible flowers (if using). Serve immediately with a Chocolate Mascarpone Cake on the side.

RUM | Whipped White Chocolate | Pineapple Crystals | Pineapple Meringue

SERVES 8

Pineapple Crystals

1 lb (500 g) frozen pineapple chunks

Place the pineapple into a colander, put a dish with a heavy weight on top (i.e. canned goods), and another container underneath the colander to collect the pineapple water (make sure the colander does not sit directly in the juice). Let it sit at room temperature for 2 hours to partly thaw, then transfer to the refrigerator to thaw completely (overnight). Pour the pineapple water into a shallow plastic container and freeze until solid (overnight is best).

Whipped White Chocolate

3.6 oz (100 g) white chocolate, finely chopped

1 cup (250 mL) whipping cream

Place the chocolate in a tall and narrow container. Bring the whipping cream to a boil in a saucepan. Remove from the heat and pour over the chocolate. Blend with an immersion blender until well combined.

Store in the refrigerator until the mixture is cooled (about 35°F/2°C).

Just before serving, whip the mixture into a soft mousse consistency (medium peaks) using an electric mixer fitted with a whip attachment.

Chocolate Pineapple Meringue

4 Tbsp (60 mL) egg whites (about 2 large)

2 Tbsp (30 mL) Fruit Water (use pineapple, see page 190)

4 Tbsp (60 g) granulated sugar

1 vanilla bean, seeds scraped

3 Tbsp (25 g) icing sugar

1 Tbsp (8 g) unsweetened cocoa powder

Preheat the oven to 250°F (120°C). Using an electric mixer fitted with a whip attachment, whip the egg whites to medium peaks. Add the pineapple water a little at a time.

Mix the sugar with the vanilla seeds. Add to the egg whites and continue whipping until stiff peaks form.

Sift the icing sugar and cocoa powder together. Using a rubber spatula, fold this into the egg white mixture. Using a piping bag fitted with a round tip, pipe 1 inch (2.5 cm) rounds onto a baking tray lined with a silicon mat.

Bake in the preheated oven for 40 minutes. Reduce the heat to 200°F

(100°C) and bake for another 1 hour. Remove from the oven and let the meringues cool on a wire rack. Store in an airtight container.

Assembly

8 chilled cocktail glasses

4 Tbsp (60 mL) freshly diced pineapple

1 Tbsp (15 mL) toasted coconut

1 recipe Alcohol Gel, (use white rum, see page 185)

8 sprigs mint

Using a fork, scrape the frozen Pineapple Crystals into small shavings and spoon approximately 1 Tbsp (15 mL) into each glass. Spoon some white rum gel alongside the Pineapple Crystals. Spoon or pipe a dollop of Whipped White Chocolate on half a spoon and fill the other half with the diced pineapple. Sprinkle with some toasted coconut and add a sprig of mint. Serve immediately with a few Chocolate Pineapple Meringues on the side.

GIN | Dark Chocolate Consommé
| Semi-Candied Kalamata Olives | Chocolate Olive Madeleine   SERVES 8

Chocolate Consommé

½ cup (100 g) granulated sugar

4 cups + 2 Tbsp (1 L + 30 mL) water, divided

1 cup (120 g) cocoa nibs
    (see page 202 for resources)

2 vanilla beans, seeds scraped

Combine the sugar and 2 Tbsp (30 mL) of the water in a saucepan over medium heat. Cook until it lightly caramelizes. Add the cocoa nibs, vanilla seeds, pods, and the remaining water to stop the caramel from cooking. Make sure all the sugar is dissolved.

Remove from the heat and cover with a tight-fitting lid. Allow it to infuse for 3 hours (the longer the infusion, the stronger the mix).

Strain the mixture into a tall and narrow container through a fine mesh sieve and discard the solids. Line the sieve with a coffee filter and strain again. Discard the filter along with any remaining solids. Let this sit in the refrigerator for approximately 8 hours or until all of the impurities have settled at the bottom of the container.

Carefully transfer the mixture into another container, making sure none of the impurities are transferred. Set aside in the refrigerator until ready to serve.

Semi-Candied Kalamata Olives

1½ cup (300 g) granulated sugar

1 cup (250 mL) water

1½ cup (200 g) pitted kalamata olives

Combine the sugar, water, and kalamata olives in a saucepan. Bring to a boil. Remove from the heat, cover with a tight-fitting lid, and allow it to infuse for at least 1 day (several days is best).

Before serving, drain the olives in a colander and pat them dry with a few sheets of paper towel. The candy process can be done ahead of time as the olives will keep for several weeks in the refrigerator.

Chocolate Olive Madeleines

1⅓ cup (200 g) all-purpose flour

1 cup + 3 Tbsp (150 g) icing sugar

1 Tbsp (15 mL) baking powder

1 large egg

1 vanilla bean, seeds scraped

zest of 1 lemon

zest of 1 orange

1 cup (250 g) unsalted butter, melted

1.6 oz (45 g) white chocolate, melted

½ cup (70 g) Semi-Candied Kalamata
    Olives, finely chopped

Preheat the oven to 325°F (165°C). Sift the flour, icing sugar, and baking powder together into a bowl. Add the egg, vanilla seeds, lemon and orange zest, butter, chocolate, and olives. Stir well to combine. Evenly pipe or spoon the mixture into 1¾ inch (4.5 cm) flexible silicon moulds or muffin tins.

Bake for approximately 15 to 20 minutes in the preheated oven. Remove from the moulds and let them cool on a wire rack. Store in an airtight container.

Assembly

1½ cup (375 mL) Chocolate
    Consommé

½ cup (125 mL) gin

crushed ice

16 Crystallized White Chocolate
    Sticks (see page 186)

8 chilled cocktail glasses

8 edible flowers (optional)

In a bar shaker, combine the Chocolate Consommé, gin, and ice. Shake vigorously. Strain into the glasses and garnish with some Semi-Candied Kalamata Olives, Crystallized White Chocolate Sticks and an edible flower (if using). Serve immediately with a Chocolate Olive Madeleine on the side.

All foodstuffs have

the same gastronomical potential

— imagination is the only limiting factor.

2007 LIMITED RELEASE 'ORIGIN' COLLECTION:
MODENA – STRAWBERRY EMULSION, GELÉE & AGED BALSAMIC

appendices

WINE PAIRING | A₁W

Much of the literature on food and wine pairing either avoids the topic of wine with chocolate or considers the pairing of these two elements unsuitable. Indeed, the pairing of wine and chocolate can be risky at best, but there are solutions to make it more successful. One of the main problems is not in the differences between these two elements, but rather in what they have in common: tannin. If you have ever bit into a grape seed, tannin is the woody taste and astringency left in your mouth.

Tannins are a type of polyphenol that are soluble in water, and provide both astringent and bitter tastes. In wine production, tannins and other polyphenols are present in the skin, seeds, and stems of grapes, and also in the wood of oak casks, which are often used to age the wine.

Polyphenols are also important in chocolate, as they add to the chocolate color and flavor. Unprocessed cocoa beans are typically high in tannins. Like wine, the cocoa beans go through a fermentation process that reduces the natural level of tannins. They may also go through a process called "dutching," where an alkaline (potassium carbonate) is added to the fermented cocoa beans to increase their pH level and dissolve some of the tannins. This process reduces the bitterness of the chocolate and also increases the brown color of the remaining tannins. The oxidation of polyphenols during the drying of the fermented cocoa beans also produces much of the brown color in chocolate.

However, when the tannins of wine and chocolate are combined, they create a very astringent flavor, sometimes accompanied by a bitter aftertaste and, in most, a very unpleasant puckering sensation in the mouth and back of the throat. Winemakers have a good degree of control over tannin levels and use specific juice extraction techniques. Specifically, the grapes can be pressed very gently or very harshly resulting in a juice with little or a lot of tannin. Typically, for red wines, contact with the grape skin is longer, the crushing of grapes more violent, and barrel aging is longer, which results in a wine with stronger tannin.

Since white wines are made with minimal skin contact, there's almost no tannin associated with the grapes. Some tannin may results from oak aging, but in much lower levels than the tannins associated with red wines. Some white wines exhibit signs of astringency, but this is mostly found in Rhone whites and the richest Chardonnay.

A basic guideline to consider when pairing wine and food (with or without chocolate) is either to match a rich, strongly flavored dish with an equally rich, powerful wine, or conversely, to contrast a strongly flavored dish with a light, acidic wine. Here are a few factors to consider:

TANNIN: Select a red wine that is low in tannin. Typically, wines intended to be drunk young have little tannin, whereas an older, aged wine requires a lot of tannin to improve over the years. Select white wines that are not aged in oak casks.

FLAVOR: As a starting point, we suggest trying to match certain flavors in the wine with similar characteristics in the food. For example, experiment with the chocolate and berry notes of a Pinot Noir with that of a dish made with dark chocolate and fruits such as the "Duck with Chocolate Port Reduction, Spiced Almond crumb, and Stewed Cherries" (page 62). (Refer to the list of Leading Varietals on page 181 for more specific flavors and aromas.) Keep in mind that every wine has its own distinct taste and aroma. The same wine will taste different when combined with different food as the elements in the wine interact with those in the food. This metamorphosis will result in very different taste sensations; some may be great while others may not be as positive. Experimentation is the key to new discoveries.

BODY: The body, or weight, of the wine should be considered. Typically, a full-bodied wine will pair better with a dish of bold flavors such as braised or stewed meats.

AMOUNT: Chocolate in savory cuisine should be thought of as more of a spice, as an underlying element rather than a bold, main ingredient. Too much chocolate will make a savory dish too sweet and/or cloying and difficult to pair.

ACIDITY/SWEETNESS: The level of acidity in both wine and food should be considered. An acidic wine, such as Sauvignon Blanc, can help to balance a rich or spicy dish. Note that a premium white chocolate is sweeter than premium darks, but contains a lot of dairy ingredients and cocoa butter. Higher percentage dark chocolate is bitter, some are even acidic and the amount of cocoa butter in the chocolate can vary from moderate to high. A sweeter wine is typically best matched with a high-acid food, whereas sweet foods tend to alter a wine's flavors and make dry wines taste flat and insipid.

Spirits are sometimes very good partners to chocolate. Try bourbon, for example, as an aperitif with savory chocolate bites. This sweet American corn-based Kentucky whiskey with its vanilla and butterscotch flavors works very well with chocolate. Experiment with aged rum, especially dark Caribbean rums made from sugar cane juice or molasses. Armagnac, the French distilled grape spirit with its pruny and nutty flavors is another good choice. Or try some eau-de-vie—crystal clear, dry spirits made from raspberries, cherries, pears, and other tree fruits.

Each variety of grape—and hence each wine—has certain characteristic flavors. Following is an at-a-glance chart of the leading table wine varietals and their basic taste/aroma notes. Depending on the region the grape is grown and the vinification process used to make the wine, the same varietal will have distinct tastes and/or aromas notes. So if you are looking to purchase a particular wine for a specific taste/aroma profile, make sure that such wine indeed has such characteristics before purchasing.

For more information and notes on leading sweet wine varietals, please refer to our first book Wild Sweets: Exotic Dessert & Wine Pairing, pages 41-43 and 55.

Leading White Table Wines

Chardonnay: *apple, pear, pineapple, melon, lemon. Typically has a smooth character, is rich & buttery or light and steely and/or oak-aged.*

Sauvignon Blanc: *flowering currant, gooseberry, lemon, lime, dill. Typically crisp, very dry, pungent and refreshing in character.*

Riesling: *peaches, apricots, honey and apples. Typically dry to slightly sweet, spicy and delicate in character.*

Gewürztraminer: *ginger, cinnamon, lychee, rose, clove, nutmeg. Typically heavier, seemingly sweet and aromatic.*

Suggested Dish Pairing*

Crab | Halibut | Salmon | Scallops | Tuna | Duck

Prawn | Scallops | Shrimp

Scallops | Crab | Pork

Prawn | Tuna | Pork

Leading Red Table Wines

Cabernet Sauvignon: *blackcurrant, vanilla, spice, black cherries, and raspberry. Soft to heavy tannins and full-bodied.*

Pinot Noir: *raspberries, strawberries, cherries, cranberries, roses, plums, chocolate, figs, and prunes. This wine offers distinct characteristics—depending on its age and origin—from simple to complex and extremely silky in texture.*

Shiraz: *blackberries, raspberries, chocolate, plums. Typically soft tannins and full-bodied.*

Merlot: *black cherry, raspberry, black currant, mint. Typically soft tannins and smooth character.*

Suggested Dish Pairing*

Lamb | Duck | Beef

Salmon | Tuna | Beef | Pork | Duck

Beef | Duck | Lamb

Scallops | Shrimp | Prawn | Tuna | Duck | Lamb | Salmon

see index for recipe page number

Cultivation of the mind
is as necessary as food to the body

– Marcus Tullius Cicero

BASIC RECIPES | A₂B

Chocolate Bases

White Chocolate

3.6 oz (100 g) white chocolate, chopped

1 cup (250 mL) whipping cream

Milk Chocolate

3.2 oz (90 g) milk chocolate, chopped

1 cup (250 mL) whipping cream

Dark Chocolate

1.9 oz (50 g) 70% dark chocolate, chopped

1 cup (250 mL) whipping cream

Place the chocolate in a tall and narrow container. Bring the whipping cream to a boil in a saucepan. Remove from the heat and pour on top of chocolate.

Blend with and immersion blender until well combined. Let it cool, then store in the refrigerator up to 4 days.

Gelatin Mix

1 Tbsp (15 mL) gelatin powder

4 Tbsp (60 mL) cold water

Combine the gelatin and water in a microwavable container. Allow the gelatin to bloom for 5 minutes. Heat the mixture in the microwave for 20 to 30 seconds, then let it set a room temperature. Cover the container with a lid and store in the refrigerator for up to 1 week.

Chocolate Milks

White Chocolate

5.9 oz (165 g) white chocolate

4 cups (1 L) water

Milk Chocolate

5.9 oz (165 g) milk chocolate

4 cups (1 L) water

Place the chocolate in a tall and narrow container. Bring the water to a boil in a saucepan. Remove from the heat and pour on top of chocolate. Blend with an immersion blender until well combined. Let it cool in the refrigerator. Skim and discard the cocoa butter that rises to the surface. Refrigerate for up to 1 week.

Alcohol Gel

4 tsp (20 mL) Gelatin Mix (see recipe this page)

1 cup (250 mL) alcohol (if using Kahlua, use only half of the Gelatin Mix)

Place the Gelatin Mix in a heatproof bowl and melt briefly over a double boiler. Remove from the heat, add the alcohol, and mix with a rubber spatula. Transfer the mixture into a container. Cover with a tight-fitting lid and refrigerate until it forms a gel (overnight is best) or for up to 3 days.

Caramel Dust

¾ cup + 3 Tbsp (180 g) granulated sugar

1 Tbsp (15 mL) corn syrup

4 Tbsp (60 mL) water

2 Tbsp (30 g) butter

Combine the sugar, corn syrup, and water in a saucepan. Cook over high heat until the mixture is caramel in color. Remove from the heat. Add the butter and mix until completely incorporated.

Pour the caramel onto a silicon mat and let cool at room temperature until completely hard. Break the caramel into small shards. Grind the shards to a fine powder in a food processor. Store in an airtight container.

NOTE: to make a nut dust, add 3 Tbsp (20 g) roasted nuts right after you add the butter. Mix until completely incorporated, then continue with the procedure.

Caramelized Nuts

½ cup (100 g) granulated sugar

¾ cup (100 g) nuts (pistachio, almonds, walnuts, pecans, etc.)

7 Tbsp (105 mL) water

Preheat the oven to 350°F (180°C). Combine the sugar, nuts, and water in a saucepan and bring to a boil. Boil for 1 to 2 minutes, then remove from the heat and strain. Discard the liquid.

Spread the nuts on a baking tray lined with a silicon mat or paper. Bake in the preheated oven until golden brown (10 to 15 minutes). Cool and store in an airtight container.

NOTE: For a crumb application, grind the cooled caramelized nuts in the food processor.

Pastry Cream

2 cups (500 mL) milk

4 Tbsp (60 g) granulated sugar

6 Tbsp (45 g) flan powder

4 Tbsp (60 g) granulated sugar

2 large eggs

Bring the milk and 4 Tbsp (60 g) of the sugar to a boil in a saucepan.

In a stainless steel bowl, mix together the remaining sugar and flan powder. Crack the eggs on top and whisk to a light lemony color. Slowly pour the hot milk overtop of the egg mixture, constantly whisking. Pour the mixture back into the saucepan, whisking the whole time, and cook on the stove until it boils. Continue cooking for 1 minute, then remove from the heat and pour into a clean container. Press plastic wrap right on top of the pastry cream; using a sharp knife poke some holes in the plastic to let the steam out. Let this cool, then store in the refrigerator until needed.

Milk Chocolate Frozen Pear Mousse

7 Tbsp (105 mL) Pear Purée (see recipe this page)

1 large egg

6 Tbsp (90 mL) egg yolks (about 4 large)

2 Tbsp (30 g) granulated sugar

12.7 oz (350 g) milk chocolate, melted

¾ cup + 2 Tbsp (205 mL) whipping cream, whipped into soft peaks

Whisk the pear purée, egg, egg yolks, and sugar in a stainless steel bowl over a double boiler. Whisk continuously until the mixture reaches 185°F (85°C). Remove from the heat and allow it to cool to 98°F (37°C).

Whisk in the melted chocolate and ¼ of the whipped cream. Add the remaining whipped cream and gently fold with a rubber spatula.

Line a 10 x 6 inch (25 x 15 cm) jellyroll pan with plastic wrap. Pour the mousse into the pan and transfer into the freezer. Once frozen cut into desired shapes and follow recipe directions.

Fruit & Vegetable Purée/Juice

For fruit and vegetables with edible peels (tree fruit such as apples and pears or vegetables such as carrots and beets), thoroughly wash the skin. Cut fruit in quarters and vegetables into chucks. Remove any large stones, but small pits, seeds, and skin can be puréed. For fruit with inedible peels (melons and citrus fruits) remove the skin. For fruits with many seeds (passion, pomegranate) crush the seeds using a rubber spatula over a stainless steel strainer.

Purée in a fruit juicer, following the operating instructions. Use the resulting purée as is. You can slightly sweeten fruit purée with a bit of corn syrup (up to 10%) if you wish to freeze it. Frozen purée can be stored up to 1 year.

If using frozen fruits or vegetables, you must first thaw overnight in the refrigerator. If you have a juicer, pass the thawed fruits or vegetables through and use as is. If not, use a food processor to purée the fruits or vegetables, then strain through a sieve.

Crystallized White Chocolate Sticks

3.6 oz (100 g) white chocolate, tempered

2 cups (500 g) granulated sugar

food color optional

Spread half of the sugar as evenly as possible on a tray. Place the tempered chocolate in a piping bag and pipe straight lines of the chocolate over the sugar. After a few lines stop and cover the top of each line with some of the sugar from the remaining half. Continue piping until all the chocolate and sugar is used up. Let the chocolate sit until completely hard, then remove the sticks and store in an airtight container in a cool dry place. The sticks will keep for several weeks and the sugar can be reused to make more.

For specific tempering techniques, please refer to page 146 – 147 in *Wild Sweets: Exotic Dessert & Wine Pairings*.

Brioche

3 Tbsp (45 mL) milk, lukewarm

one ¼ oz (7 g) package dry active
   yeast

3⅓ cup (500 g) all-purpose flour

3 Tbsp (45 g) granulated sugar

2 tsp (10 mL) salt

6 large eggs

1 cup (250 g) unsalted butter, room
   temperature

Place the warm milk in the bowl of
the electric mixer, sprinkle the yeast
overtop, stir, and let it sit for
2 minutes.

Add all the dry ingredients and knead
the dough with a dough hook until a
ball is formed.

Add the eggs one at a time and
continue kneading for approximately
15 minutes until a smooth and elastic
dough has formed. At this stage add
the butter in 4 stages, making sure it
is completely incorporated after each
addition before adding the next. Once
all the butter is added, beat for about
5 minutes. Place the brioche in a large,
lightly buttered bowl. Cover the bowl
with a clean cloth and place in a warm
area without drafts. Let it sit until the
dough has doubled in size. Punch
the dough down and continue in one
of the two following ways: shape
the dough and let it sit again until it
doubles in size, brush it with an egg
wash and bake it; or you can leave it
in the bowl, cover it with plastic wrap,
and leave in the refrigerator overnight
(about 8 hours). Bake at 375 to 400°F
(190 to 200°C) for 35 to 40 minutes.
Follow the remaining instructions
below.

To make Brioche – Bread Tuiles

Place the baked Brioche (you can also
use a store-bought, sweet-type bread)
in the freezer until hard but not frozen
(about 1 hour).

Preheat the oven to 250°F (120°C).
Line a baking tray with a silicon mat
or paper. Using a sharp serrated
knife or electric meat slicer, slice the
hardened bread into slices as thin as
possible. Place the slices on the baking
tray and bake until dry and crispy
(for a curved look, lay the pieces in a
terrine-type mould). Once cool, store
in an airtight container.

Simple Syrup

1 cup (250 mL) water

1¼ cup (250 g) granulated sugar

Combine the water and sugar in
a saucepan and bring to a boil. As
soon as it boils, remove from the
heat. (If boiled longer, the syrup will
become sweeter as water evaporates.)
Pour the syrup into a clean plastic
container with a tight fitting lid.
Seal the container immediately to
trap the steam and protect against
re-crystallization. Cool at room
temperature, then refrigerate until
needed. This syrup will keep in the
refrigerator for several weeks.

Herb Oil

½ cup (125 mL) grapeseed oil

2 oz (60 g) herbs (leaves and stalks
   of basil, tarragon, etc.)

pinch ascorbic acid
   (see note page 188)

Pour the oil into a saucepan and bring
to a boil. Place the herbs and ascorbic
acid together in a food processor. Turn
on the motor and slowly pour the
oil over the herb mixture. Continue
mixing for at least 1 minute, or until
all the chlorophyll has been released
(the mixture should be deep green).
Pour the mixture into a tall and
narrow container and let it rest in the
refrigerator until the oil and solids
separate and form a sediment at the
bottom of the container. Carefully
pour the oil off without disturbing
the sediments. Discard the sediments.
The oil will keep for 1 week in the
refrigerator.

Vanilla Oil

½ cup (125 mL) grapeseed oil

1 whole vanilla bean, seeds scraped

Pour the grapeseed oil into a container
with a tight fitting lid. Add the vanilla
seeds and pod and let infuse in the
refrigerator for at least 3 days. Oil can
be kept for 4 weeks in the refrigerator.

Herb Emulsion

⅓ cup (75 g) granulated sugar

1 tsp (5 mL) powdered pectin

5 Tbsp (75 mL) water

1.9 oz (50 g) herbs (leaves and stalks of basil, tarragon, etc.)

3 Tbsp (45 mL) grapeseed oil

pinch of ascorbic acid (see note below)

Combine the sugar and pectin in a saucepan or a microwaveable bowl. Stir in the water and bring to a boil.

Combine the herbs, oil, and ascorbic acid in a food processor and pulse a few times. With the motor running, slowly pour the hot syrup over the herb mixture so that it emulsifies. Continue mixing for at least 1 minute, or until all chlorophyll has been released (the mixture should be deep green). Strain the emulsion through cheesecloth, squeezing hard to remove all the liquid. Discard the herb remnants and refrigerate the emulsion in a small airtight container or, better yet, covered with plastic wrap pressed tightly against the emulsion. The emulsion will keep for 3 to 4 days in the refrigerator.

NOTE: Ascorbic Acid

Ascorbic acid is available in health food stores where you will find it in powder form or as vitamin C pills, which can be ground to a powder. Ascorbic acid is an antioxidant and naturally prevents herbs from turning brown when exposed to air.

Brown Butter

Place the butter in a heavy saucepan over low heat. When the butter starts to foam, milk solids at the bottom of the pan start to turn brown (but are not burned), and the mixture has a pleasant nutty odor. Once it reaches this point, remove from the heat. Use as directed in recipe.

Hot Fruit Gelée

1 cup (250 mL) Fruit or Vegetable Purée (see page 186)

1 tsp (5 mL) agar powder

pinch of citric acid (optional)

1½ tsp (7.5 mL) Gelatin Mix (see page 185)

4 Tbsp (60 mL) corn syrup (for sweet gelée)

Pour the juice into a tall and narrow container, add the agar powder and citric acid (if using) and blitz immediately with an immersion blender until well combined. Transfer the mixture into a saucepan (add the corn syrup at this point, if using). Stir constantly and bring to a boil. Continue cooking until the mixture starts to thicken. Remove from the heat, add the gelatin, stir to dissolve, and immediately pour into a container or thinly onto a silicon mat to make 'sheets'. Let it set at room temperature. Keep the gelée warm or store in the refrigerator.

Fruit Gelée / Jelly

½ cup (125 mL) Fruit or Vegetable Purée (see page 186)

1 Tbsp (15 mL) Gelatin Mix (see page 185)

Heat 4 Tbsp (60 mL) of the purée in the microwave. Add the Gelatin Mix and stir until completely dissolved. Add the remaining purée and stir again. Transfer into a shallow container. Cover and let it set in the refrigerator, overnight is best.

Lemon Confit

4 lemons

1¼ cup (250 g) granulated sugar

½ cup (125 mL) water

Peel the lemons (ensure that all the white pith is removed), then section with a sharp knife.

Bring the sugar and water to a boil in a saucepan and add the lemons. Reduce the heat to low and simmer for 15 to 20 minutes. Remove from the heat, cover with plastic wrap and let it sit for a couple of hours (for the best results, let it sit overnight in the refrigerator).

Fruit Chips

Fresh fruit (strawberries, oranges, etc)

Preheat oven to 200°F (95°C). For the best results, use a food dehydrator set at 135°F (58°C) and dry for approximately 2 hours. Quickly wash the fruit under running water and remove the stems and any blemishes.

Line a baking tray with a silicon mat. Slice the fruit into ¼ inch (6 mm) thick slices using a sharp knife, mandoline slicer, or electric slicer. Lay the slices flat without touching and bake for approximately 1 hour in the preheated oven. Turn the slices over and continue baking for another hour or until dry. Store in an airtight container.

Fruit Coulis

1 cup (250 mL) Fruit Purée (see page 186)

2 Tbsp (30 mL) freshly squeezed lemon juice

1– 2% aroma, by weight, optional (vanilla bean, fresh ginger, etc.)

¼ cup + 1 tsp (55 g) granulated sugar

¾ tsp (3.75 mL) powdered pectin or xanthan gum

Bring the Fruit Purée, juice, and aroma (if using) to a quick boil in a saucepan. Remove from the heat, cover with a tight fitting lid or plastic wrap, and let it infuse for at least 1 hour (the longer, the stronger the infusion). Strain and discard the aroma. Add the sugar and pectin (mixed together beforehand) and bring the mixture to a boil while stirring at all times. Continue cooking until the mixture reaches the consistency of whipping cream. Alternately, replace the pectin with xanthan gum and proceed as above; the cooking time will be much shorter. Cool the mixture and refrigerate until ready to serve.

Fruit Foam

1 cup (150 mL) Fruit Water (see page 190)

2 tsp (10 mL) lecithin (see resouces page 202)

Place all ingredients in a tall and narrow container and blend with an immersion blender until a generous foam forms on top of the liquid. Serve as per recipe specifications.

Strawberry Sorbet

¼ cup + 2 Tbsp (80 g) granulated sugar

¼ tsp (1.25 mL) powdered pectin

6 Tbsp (90 mL) water

1 cup (250 mL) Fruit Purée (use strawberries, see page 186)

In a saucepan, combine the sugar and powdered pectin. Add the water and bring the mixture to a boil, either on the stovetop or in a microwave. Make sure the mixture is transparent; if it is milky, the pectin is not completely "cooked." Stir in fruit juice and mix thoroughly. If necessary, strain and discard the solids. Refrigerate the mixture overnight. Churn using a regular ice cream machine and keep frozen. Sorbet will keep up to 1 week.

Green Apple Skin Sorbet

¼ cup (50 g) granulated sugar

¼ tsp (1.25 mL) powdered pectin

⅓ cup + 2 Tbsp (105 mL) water

zest and juice of ½ lime

5 large organic Granny Smith apples, skin only with ¾ inch (2 cm) flesh

In a saucepan, combine the sugar and pectin. Add the water and lime zest and bring to a boil. Remove from the heat, strain, and add the lime juice. Place the apple skin in a high-speed blender and pour the syrup on top. Blend until the mixture reaches a uniform purée. Refrigerate the mixture overnight. Churn using a regular ice cream machine and keep frozen. Sorbet will keep up to 1 week.

Chocolate Puff Pastry

¾ cup + 1 Tbsp (200 g) unsalted butter

4 Tbsp + 1 tsp (35 g) unsweetened cocoa powder

1⅔ cup (250 g) all-purpose flour

1 tsp (5 mL) salt

½ cup (125 mL) water

3 Tbsp (45 g) unsalted butter, melted

Combine the first butter with the cocoa powder in an electric mixer bowl fitted with a paddle attachment. Mix until well combined. Form the butter into a 3 inch (8 cm) square, wrap it in plastic wrap, and store in the refrigerator for at least 1 hour or until needed.

Combine the flour, salt, water, and melted butter in an electric mixer bowl fitted with a dough hook. Mix on low speed until the dough begins to form, then turn to the second-lowest speed and mix for another 3 minutes or until a well-developed dough has formed. Remove from the bowl and knead into a ball. Let it rest for about 30 minutes on a lightly floured board covered with a clean cloth.

Using a sharp knife, cut an X on the top of the dough ball, then push down each quarter (the dough should appear as an X). The middle of the dough should be twice as thick as the ends.

Place the cocoa powder butter in the center of the X, then take the dough ends and fold them on top of the butter (work clockwise to cover the cocoa butter completely). Roll the dough out to 3 x 9 inches (8 x 23 cm), dust off any flour, then fold the dough into thirds. Indent the dough with 1 finger mark, cover the dough with plastic wrap, and let it rest in the refrigerator for 30 minutes. Remove the dough from the refrigerator and rotate the dough 90 degrees from the finger mark. Each time the dough is turned you will indent the dough again (so you can keep track of how many turns) for a total of 4 turns. Either use straight away, or let it rest in the refrigerator overnight before using.

Preheat the oven to 375°F (190°C). Roll the dough out to 8 inches wide and ¼ inch thick (20 x 6 mm) and cut into ¼ inch (6 mm) strips. Place the strips on a baking tray lined with a silicon mat or paper and bake for until done (about 5 minutes). Remove from the oven and let it cool at room temperature. Store in an airtight container. Unused portions of the dough can be stored in the freezer for several weeks.

To make Sticks: Preheat the oven to 350°F (180°C). Roll the dough out to 8 wide and ¼ inch thick (20 x 0.5 cm) and cut ¼ inch (0.5 cm) strips. Place on a baking tray lined with silicon paper or mat and bake for approximately 10 minutes or until done.

Fruit Water

1 lb (450 g) frozen fruit

Place the frozen fruit in a colander, put a dish with a heavy weight on top (i.e. canned goods) and another container underneath the colander to collect the fruit juice (make sure the colander does not sit directly in the juice). Let the frozen fruit sit at room temperature for 2 hours to partly thaw, then transfer into the refrigerator to thaw completely (overnight). The water may be used for applications such as fruit gelées, crystals, soups, or wherever a clear fruit juice is required.

Broiled Tomatoes

Tomatoes (yellow, strawberry, cherry, grape)

salt & pepper to taste

Briefly roast the tomatoes under the broiler until the skin shrivels (approximately 1 minute) and sprinkle with some salt and pepper to taste.

Roasted Onions

16 onions (shallots, pearl onions, small cipollinis)

3 Tbsp (45 mL) olive oil

salt and pepper to taste

aroma (fresh thyme, rosemary, etc) (optional)

Preheat the oven to 350°F (180°C). Place the onions in the middle of a large piece of aluminum foil. Drizzle the olive oil overtop, season to taste, and evenly distribute the aroma (if using). Crimp the foil over the onions to form a sealed pouch and roast in the preheated oven until they are soft, but still hold their shape. Alternately, place the onions, along with seasonings, in a sealed bag and cook in a 150°F (65°C) agitated water bath (see page 36) for approximately 60 minutes or until done.

Vegetable Stock

1 onion, peeled and cut into quarters

1 stalk celery, cut into 6 to 8 pieces

1 carrot, cut into 6 to 8 pieces

4 white button mushrooms, cut into quarters

1 clove garlic

3 sprigs fresh thyme

8 peppercorns, whole

4 cups (1 L) water

Combine all the ingredients in a saucepan. Bring to a boil, then simmer for 20 minutes. For faster results, use a pressure cooker, bring to pressure, cook for one minute under pressure, remove from the heat source and let it infuse/cook while the pressure comes down on its own. Strain (make sure not to press on the vegetables to keep the stock as clear as possible). Store in the refrigerator or freezer.

Mushroom Emulsion

1 oz (30 g) dried mushrooms

1 cup (250 mL) hot water

1 Tbsp (15 mL) freshly squeezed lemon juice

¼ tsp (1.25 mL) xanthan gum

1 tsp (5 mL) powdered pectin

2 Tbsp (30 mL) olive oil

Rehydrate the dried mushrooms (wild, or cultivated, or a mix of both) in the hot water for approximately 30 minutes. Squeeze the mushrooms to release all of the water; reserve the mushrooms and water. Measure ½ cup (125 mL) of the mushroom water and place in a tall and narrow container. Add the lemon juice, xanthan, and pectin and mix immediately with an immersion blender until well combined. Transfer the mixture into a saucepan, add the oil and bring to a boil. Continue cooking, whisking constantly, until the mixture starts to thicken. Place the mushrooms in a food processor, add the hot mixture, and continue mixing until a thick, homogenous paste is reached. Keep warm or store in the refrigerator.

Wild sweets

DC DUBY Wild Sweets is an innovative chocolate design atelier located in beautiful British Columbia (Vancouver, Canada). Its critically-acclaimed virtual boutique is located at **dcduby.com.** Wild Sweets' unique products and novel concepts reflect the past but also look to the future. Its goal is to contribute at the sensory level, to provide pleasure and to evoke emotions. The virtual boutique features luxurious chocolate gifts (such as CocoArt) as well as simpler, deliciously designed chocolates and other confections. Wild Sweets' virtual boutique reflects the Dubys' perspective on the use of technology as an alternative to the traditional street boutique; it's a dynamic, interactive, and multi-sensory site that makes extensive use of audio and visual materials.

Inspired by Nature The Dubys are known for taking calculated, well-researched risks, but they never lose sight of their commitment to superlative design and taste experiences. The name, Wild Sweets, reflects their rational: blending the exotic with the familiar, an element of surprise with a sense of comfort. The Dubys believe that "everything works until proven it doesn't" and they continually reinvent and question themselves on their food and product preparation and presentation. They do not take tradition for granted and devote several months a year experimenting in their design atelier with an intricate and ever-expanding list of both classic and unusual ingredients. They continue to find ways to innovate by using non-traditional exotic and wild ingredients to create unique sweets while taking sweet inspired techniques and ingredients to create their own approach and perspective of savory cuisine.

Guided by Science Dominique and Cindy have a particular interest in scientific research, with the aim of developing and implementing new techniques to create modern tastes and textures. Their true passion lies in expanding the palette of flavors and ingredients available to chefs. They believe that science and psychology are an integral part of a modern food experience. Their methodology is based on the application of scientific principles and techniques aimed at better understanding and improve small-scale artisan food production. They work on a regular basis with food scientists to research, develop and implement techniques to create new tastes and textures. The results of their work include many novel concepts including an annual limited-release chocolate collection. Their unique science-based approach is also showcased in their multi-sensory, laboratory-like Wild Sweets Tasting Theatre that offers "edutaining" and interactive sweet, savory and pairing sessions.

Crafted by Art While there's a strong scientific foundation to their work, the Dubys do not believe in putting science above art. They view food as an art form and have won many awards at some of the world's most prestigious culinary art competitions. Dominique and Cindy

highly value the cognitive or brain-based aspect of eating and perceiving food through multi-sensory stimulation, especially with intense flavors and powerful aromas, but also with contrasting textures and vibrant colors. They take inspiration from various fields, from architecture to painting. They continuously search for, design, and implement various art techniques such as thermoforming, stamping, embossing, design transfer, and airbrushing. They play with colors based on Matching Systems, and apply artist techniques for unique strokes and brushing effects. All this results in an intricate design, colors and textures that turn an otherwise plain chocolate into a truly unique creation that can only be called 'CocoArt'.

Designed by Technology Although most of Wild Sweets' chocolates are painstakingly handcrafted in true artisan fashion, the results of their research are often implemented in the daily production of chocolates.

In the Wild Sweets kitchen, you can find unique pieces of equipment generally only used in science laboratories. For example, when the Dubys wanted to transform wine from a liquid to a powder form with the least amount of aroma loss for a chocolate bar filling, they acquired a leading Vacuum Drying Microwave system. To extract the most chlorophyll and aromatic compounds from fresh herbs for flavor emulsions and other fillings, they use high-speed centrifuges that yield beautifully clear and incredibly aromatic oils. Other "basic" pieces of equipment such as the pH metre or refractometre are also commonly used in daily production to implement standardization of all recipes and ensure consistency in every single batch.

One of the Dubys' mottos sums it up best: "A chef who stops learning is a retired chef." Dominique and Cindy are committed to continually researching art, science, and technology for new ways to provide chocolate lovers with superlative taste experiences—and to continue sharing their passion for chocolate.

THE DUBYS 'JAZZ' FOOD ART SHOWPIECE
– one of their of all-chocolate sculptures
presented during the *2003 World Pastry Cup*
team competition in Lyon, France

The preparation of good food
is merely another expression of art,
one of the joys of civilized living

- Dione Lucas

Equipment

The stores listed below provide and/or carry most of the special tools and equipment listed in this book, including: silicone mats, pastry combs, Japanese mandolines/slicers, ice cream scoops, ring moulds, thermometers, digital scales, etc.

A Cook's Wares
1-800-915-9788
www.cookswares.com

Crate & Barrel
1-800-967-6696
www.crateandbarrel.com

Dean & Deluca
1-877-826-9246
www.deandeluca.com

Home Outfitters
www.hbc.com

JB Prince
1-800-473-0577
www.jbprince.com

Macy's
1-800-289-6229
www.macys.com

Sur La Table
1-800-243-0852
www.surlatable.com

Williams-Sonoma
1-877-812-6235
www.williams-sonoma.com

Ingredients

DC DUBY Wild Sweets
604-277-6102
www.dcduby.com

Bulk chocolate, chocolate and caramel confits, cocoa nibs, cocoa butter, egg white powder, DC DUBY Wild Sweets Elements® ingredients such as gelatin, pectin, xanthan, agar, lecithin, caramel powder, infused oils, arOma salts, gels, and more.

The stores listed below provide and/or carry other specialty ingredients such as origin chocolate, exotic oils and spices, etc.

Dean & Deluca
1-877-826-9246
www.deandeluca.com

Sur La Table
1-800-243-0852
www.surlatable.com

Photo Credits

All photography by Dominique & Cindy Duby except for portraits done by:

Rita Schurman page 8, 13, 19, and dust jacket

Linda Mitsui page 11, 15, 184, 187, 190

Patrick Hattenburger page 17, 21, 109

RESOURCES | A₄R